P

C000088891

Kenya

Part of the Langenscheidt Publishing Group

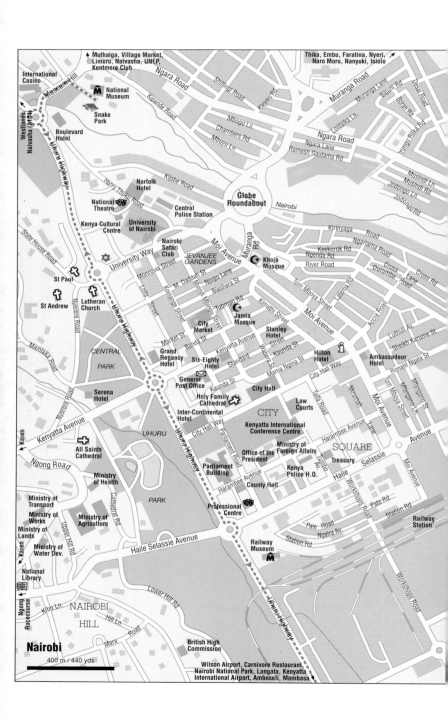

Nairobi

400 m / 440 yds

Welcome

T his is one of 133 itinerary-based *Pocket Guides* produced by the editors of Insight Guides, whose books have set the standard for visual travel guides since 1970. With top-quality photography and authoritative recommendations, this guidebook is intended to help you make the most of your stay in this incredibly varied and exciting destination. Whatever you want to do, there's a holiday to suit you in Kenya – whether you've come to see the animals on the great game plains, to snorkel in the Indian Ocean, to climb Africa's second-highest mountain, or to journey through the desert; whether you want to stay in lodges, luxury hotels or traditional safari camps.

Our experts have designed 25 itineraries (18 setting out from Nairobi and seven from Mombasa or Watamu on the coast), varying from the luxurious to the adventurous. We explain where to see elephants, lions, buffalo, rhinos, exotic birds and tropical fish; how to arrange a ride in a hot-air balloon, a ride on horseback among the game, a hike up Mount Kenya or deep-sea fishing in the Indian Ocean.

Marti Colley first got to know Kenya as a backpacker smitten by the travel bug. But, unlike her friends who went home at the end of their travels, she stayed on in Kenya, working as a consultant writer and editor for the United Nations Environment Programme in Nairobi. Even with her itchy feet, she says, she realised that Kenya was not a country to be rushed through, but rather a land to savour. *Pole pole* (slowly, slowly) is the only way to go. So if you're looking to unwind and forget the pressures of home, you've come to the right place.

All the material from previous editions of this book has been thoroughly checked and updated by Kenyan **Suzie Sardelli**, who was born on a farm in Naro Moru and now lives in Nairobi. She really got to know the country well when she worked surveying the route for the famous Safari Rally. For this edition, Suzie has added new itineraries (to Meru National Park and Lewa Wildlife Conservancy, *page 45*, and Western Kenya, *page 52*) and supplied many new entries to the sections on Accommodation, Nightlife and Eating Out.

Right: a Pokot girl near Lake Baringo

contents

Pages 2/3: wildebeest in the Maasai Mara
Pages 8/9: Samburu warrior looking towards Mt Kenya

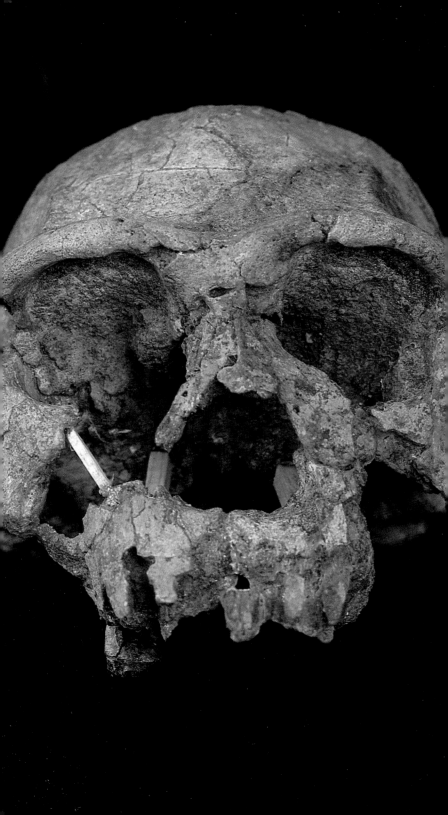

History *& Culture*

Kenya's Rift Valley is rightly named the 'Cradle of Mankind'. Clues to man's earliest history were unearthed there in the 1960s when anthropologists Mary and Louis Leakey found the remains of a large-brained hominid with gripping thumbs that put back the believed origins of man by about 1½ million years. The remains are still the object of some controversy although later finds by the Leakeys' son, Richard, seem to confirm that primitive man was around much earlier than was originally thought.

The history of the next few thousand centuries is not very clear. Kenya was on one of the major immigration routes through Africa and, beginning around 2,000 BC, successive waves of Cushitic, Bantu and Nilotic peoples passed through, bringing with them tool-making and agricultural skills.

These are the ancestors of the more than 40 different peoples who make up modern Kenya, and who have made the country a virtual paradise for archaeologists and anthropologists.

Arab Influence

In the 9th century, even as migrations continued in the interior, the coastal towns of Mombasa and Malindi were already important trade centres between India, Arabia and Africa. Their development received a boost with the emergence of Islam, which sent political and religious dissidents flocking to the south, bringing with them the Arab architecture and culture that still dominate Kenya's coast today. Trade flourished and the next five or six centuries were boom years as Mombasa, Malindi and Lamu became centres of all that was new – technology, business, literature, arts and crafts. Around this time Kiswahili, a mixture of Arabic and the vernacular, is believed to have developed.

Arab domination continued until 1498 when Vasco da Gama arrived, looking for a sea route from Portugal to India. At first the Arabs repelled his fleet from Mombasa, but he was welcomed by the sultan at Malindi, who loaded his ships with riches and gave him a guide to Calcutta. Elsewhere on the coast the Arabs had to pay bitterly for their lack of hospitality. For the next 200 years Mombasa was repeatedly attacked, reduced to rubble and rebuilt. In 1593 the Portuguese began the construction of Fort Jesus in Mombasa and over the next century consolidated their position along the coast. It wasn't until 1696 that the Arabs started to fight back successfully. In 1729 they finally drove the Portuguese out, and once again dominated trade in the area until the end of the 19th century.

Left: skull of *Homo erectus* found beside Lake Turkana
Right: Arab-Swahili tombstone from Fort Jesus, Mombasa

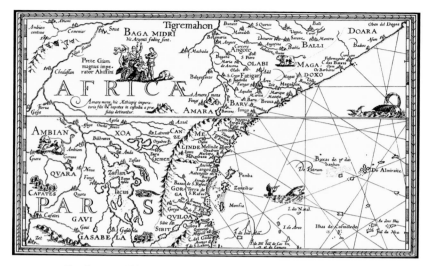

For the next 100 years the coast was ruled by the Imam of Oman except for a brief, three-year interlude from 1824 when an over-zealous British captain made Mombasa a Protectorate of the Crown of England. This was later repudiated and power passed back to Oman until the late 1880s.

By this time Oman's court had moved to Zanzibar, and the British and Germans, aware of the wealth of the East African coast, had begun trading in the region. In 1886, both Britain and Germany agreed that the Omani sultan would rule the Kenyan coast up to a depth of 16km (10 miles), but it would remain as a British Protectorate. It stayed this way until 1963 when the ruling sultan handed it over to the newly independent Kenya.

Colonials and the Interior

Until the 1880s the Kenyan interior remained closed to outsiders who were afraid of the dominant Maasai tribe and their reputation for ferocity. But Kenya could not remain inviolate for long. By 1883 Joseph Thomson had 'discovered' the Rift Valley lakes and travelled as far as Lake Victoria. Two years later, Bishop James Hannington 'found' Lake Bogoria. By this time Maasai strength had been depleted by disease and clan fighting, and the British were able to negotiate a treaty allowing them to build a railway through

the centre of Maasai grazing lands, from Mombasa to Lake Victoria. It was finally completed in 1901.

The railway was symbolic of the race to colonise Africa. Its aim was to set up communications with Uganda before the Germans and so establish British dominance in the region. The British Parliament described the scheme as a waste of both time and money and 'a lunatic

Above: a 16th-century map of the coast
Left: the Maasai meet the British, 1898

line to nowhere'. But the project went ahead anyway at a massive cost to the British taxpayer of £9,500 a mile.

To make a return on the investment, Europeans were encouraged to settle and farm the land along the railway line. This was the start of the era when renegade minor British aristocrats and other 'White Highlanders' came to start afresh in the foothills of the Aberdares, which offered the best prospects for arable development. By 1912 the Protectorate was paying its own way.

Following World War I, the British government began the Soldier Settlement Scheme, in which estates in the White Highlands were given away in a lottery or sold for peanuts to white veterans of the European campaign. The Africans who had fought alongside the Europeans were offered nothing. By the 1950s over 80,000 Europeans had settled in Kenya.

The Struggle for Freedom

Not surprisingly the native Kenyans were unhappy with government practices, which took land away from Africans to give to white settlers. In the 1920s, as increasingly repressive laws were enforced, they formed their first political parties with the ultimate aim of taking over from the British and running the country for themselves. This was the beginning of the struggle for *Uhuru* – freedom.

It was a struggle that took many years to win. After World War II, demobilised African soldiers returned to Kenya in militant frame of mind, fully trained in the use of arms and having realised that the Europeans were not all-powerful. They campaigned for changes under the leadership of Jomo Kenyatta who had lived in self-imposed exile in London for 15 years, where he had pleaded the African cause with the Colonial Secretary.

For the next seven years the calls for change became more vociferous until, frustrated by the lack of action, a guerilla movement – *Mau Mau* – was formed. Its members swore to kill those who supported the colonial regime. The first deaths – of 21 Kikuyus (Bantu-speaking farmers) loyal to the British – came in 1953 and the bloodshed continued up to 1956, by which time some 13,500 Africans and 100 Europeans had died and more than 20,000 Kikuyus were detained in special camps. The colonial government accused Kenyatta, probably unjustly, of leading the *Mau Mau* campaign and he was imprisoned until 1959. But although *Mau Mau* was effectively suppressed, it was clear that colonialism had had its day.

In 1960 the Lancaster House Conference was held in London at which it was agreed that power should be transferred to a democratically elected black government. When independence came on 12 December 1963, Jomo Kenyatta, leader of the Kikuyus, was elected president.

Right: Jomo Kenyatta speaking in Trafalgar Square, London, in 1938

Stability and Democracy

Kenyatta ruled for the next 15 years and steered Kenya towards stability and prosperity, certainly in African terms. At first, his policies brought about rapid economic growth and there was a mood of optimism for Kenya's future prosperity. By 1970 two-thirds of European-owned land had been sold to the government in obligatory land sales and was then handed over to 50,000 landless peasants as subsistence plots.

Internationally, Kenya was seen as a model of African stability and democracy. However, an elite group of profiteers had emerged who exploited their connections with the president to milk the country dry, notably through ivory trading. Kenyatta's wife, Mama Ngina, is widely thought to have been involved. Besides nepotism, Kenyatta's worst failing was his inability to accept honest criticism. Many of those who spoke out against him were detained without trial. Other critics met mysterious deaths.

On Kenyatta's death in 1978 he was succeeded by Vice President Daniel Toroitich arap Moi. During the first 10 years of his reign, Moi consolidated his hold on power through increased oppression and intolerance of political opposition. He amended the constitution to make Kenya officially a one-party state – which led to an unsuccessful coup attempt by the Air Force in 1982 – and in 1987 gave himself the power to appoint and dismiss members of the judiciary. By the end of the decade Moi had no effective political opposition. Corruption was rife and the standard of living was falling. There was growing discontent but most Kenyans were too afraid to talk.

Events came to a head in 1990 when the collapse of communism in Eastern Europe opened Kenyan eyes to the possibility of political change. At first Moi used paramilitary security units to crack down on pro-democracy demonstrations and had opposition leaders arrested and detained without trial. But the popular movement for political change continued to gain momentum and received a boost when Western powers, faced with the global recession, were forced to choose between regenerating Eastern European economies or continuing to support undemocratic African regimes. One by one, diplomatic missions announced that aid to Kenya was to be frozen until multi-party elections were held.

Yielding to external pressure, in 1992 Moi released the detainees and rescinded the constitutional one-party status. A handful of newly-formed political parties were registered to contest the 1992 general election, but they failed to agree on a joint presidential candidate, and Moi won a fresh five-year mandate. Within months, the shilling collapsed and economic hardship followed for many Kenyans.

Five years later, little had changed. The election campaign was marred by demonstrations, riots and allegations of electoral fraud. The main

Above: Daniel arap Moi, President of Kenya from 1978 to 2002

opposition leaders were placed under house arrest, the opposition parties were split along tribal lines, and Moi's KANU party once again won control.

At the start of the new Parliament, the President made promises to eradicate poverty and corruption and to stimulate the economy. In a surprise move, he made Richard Leakey head of the civil service and Cabinet Secretary, with the challenging task of clearing up corruption. But in December 2000, the Kenya Anti-Corruption Authority (KACA) suffered a setback when the High Court ruled it was not a constitutionally legal body. The Anti-Corruption and Economic Crimes Bill was thrown out of Parliament – and as a result the International Monetary Fund and World Bank refused to resume funding, which had been suspended in 1997 pending reform. In April 2001 Leakey stood down, not entirely voluntarily, from his role as sleaze-buster.

Meanwhile, Moi's KANU party was not having it all its own way. Its majority was smaller than in previous administrations, and a number of younger parliamentarians were beginning to question the party line.

With Moi obliged to stand down from the presidency, the opposition parties saw their chance to seize power in the 2002 election. Most of them combined – for the first time since the multi-party system was introduced – to form the National Rainbow Coalition (NARC), with Mwai Kibaki as their sole presidential candidate. In December 2002, Kibaki and NARC won the presidential and parliamentary elections by a landslide, giving Kenya its first new ruling party since Independence. The new government promptly implemented one of its election promises – the reintroduction of free primary education – then turned its attention to the long-standing problems of corruption.

There were few in Kenya – apart from corrupt officials, magistrates and police officers who lost their jobs in the ensuing purges – who objected to the clean-up of the political scene. But the government's next grand project, constitutional reform aimed at introducing the executive office of Prime Minister, proved more controversial. In November 2005 a referendum was held on the proposed new constitution. It divided Kenyans and brought

Above: camels are important in the lives of the Turkana people

violence between supporters of reform and their opponents, resulting in the deaths of nine people. The voting process was peaceful, but 58 percent of the voters rejected the new constitution, many of them using the referendum as a means of voicing their views on Kibaki's administration. The president promptly dismissed his entire cabinet to re-organise his government.

It remains to be seen whether Mwai Kibaki can quell the political infighting that has slowed the reform process, and hold the National Rainbow Coalition intact until the General Election due to take place in 2007.

Wildlife Preservation

The earliest hunter-gatherers had a healthy respect for wildlife and killed only to eat or as a religious ritual – to kill an animal without reason was to violate all that was sacred and to call for retribution from the powers above.

Five thousand years ago nomadic herders from Ethiopia and the Nile Valley brought domestic livestock into Kenya. They began to live in symbiosis with the indigenous hunter-gatherers, trading milk and the use of land for wildlife products and labour. These early herders accepted the right of animals other than cattle, sheep and goats to share land and water resources. Today, three-quarters of Kenya is still inhabited by herders and pastoralists.

The concept of land ownership and large-scale commercial farming was introduced when Europeans moved into the hinterland of Kenya in the late 19th century. So began Kenya's massive transformation into an environment manipulated by man.

Some modification was beneficial – such as the early burning of grasslands, which cleared the regenerating shrubs and ensured that new grass could benefit from the rain. Other modifications left lasting damage – for example, forest-clearing on steep slopes, which depleted the water table, and the over-exploitation of vulnerable species such as elephant, rhino and leopard for the pleasure of hunting and financial gain.

The development of modern medicine led to a population explosion in the early 20th century which put great pressure on natural resources, particularly wildlife. Increasing numbers of species and their habitats were threatened with extinction.

Following the mass destruction of World War II, there was worldwide concern about conserving the earth's biodiversity. Kenya was one of the first countries to take action – by conserving the environment and wildlife of the Athi River plains on the outskirts of Nairobi in the nation's first national park, gazetted in 1945. Twenty years later Kenya had one of the best systems of national parks in the world, which was one reason why the United Nations made Nairobi the base for their Environment Programme (UNEP) in the early 1970s. Today, nearly 8 percent of Kenya's land area is protected.

Left: as part of the attempt to stamp out poaching, tons of recovered ivory were burned in 1990

HISTORY HIGHLIGHTS

1.8 million BC Ancestral hominids living on the shores of Lake Turkana.

500,000 BC Cushitic, Nilotic and Bantu peoples, the ancestors of today's Kenyans, move in from all over Africa.

AD110 Diogenes the Greek records trade in Mombasa during the rule of King Muza.

900 Arrival of Islam; the beginning of the coast's golden age.

14th century Arab and Persian settlers develop coastal trade and caravan routes to the interior.

1498 Vasco da Gama arrives in Malindi, the start of Portuguese influence which ends in 1696 when Arabs besiege Fort Jesus.

1824 Captain Owen claims Kenya as a British Protectorate. Three years later control is surrendered to Oman.

1849 First European sighting of Mount Kenya by Austrian Johan Krapf.

1880 Joseph Thomson explores Maasai Land at the bequest of the British Royal Geographical Society and charts much of modern Kenya.

1886 Kenya and Uganda are assigned to the British at the Berlin Conference.

1892 Johnstone Kamau, later to change his name to Jomo Kenyatta, is born in the Highlands north of Nairobi.

1896 Construction of the 'Lunatic Line' from Mombasa to Uganda begins. It takes six years to complete.

1918 British government offers World War I veterans land in the Kenyan Highlands as part of a settlement scheme.

1922 Harry Thuku, leader of the first pan-Kenyan nationalist organisation, is arrested. Protesting Kenyans are massacred in Nairobi.

1929 Jomo Kenyatta goes to England to plead East African Association's cause.

1939 World War II: Kenya used by the British as a base and training ground for operations in Abyssinia (Ethiopia).

1944 Start of *Mau Mau*, an underground independence movement with an oath of allegiance against Britain.

1952 Simmering Kenyan nationalism. A state of emergency is called following attacks against white settlers. Kenyatta and other leaders are imprisoned.

1959 Kenyatta released and put under house arrest.

1963 Kenya gains independence; Kenyatta is first elected president.

1964 Kenya declared a republic.

1978 Daniel Toroitich arap Moi becomes president on death of Kenyatta.

1982 Attempted coup led by rebels in the Kenyan Air Force. Moi makes Kenya a one-party state.

1992 Kenyans call for political plurality. The first multi-party elections for 26 years are held. Moi re-elected, amid allegations of ballot-rigging.

1993 Kenyan shilling devalued by around 50 percent.

1997 Moi re-elected president as opposition parties are split along tribal lines.

1998 Islamic terrorists plant a car bomb near US Embassy in Nairobi, killing more than 200.

2000 Prolonged drought causes power crisis: electricity is rationed.

2001 Constitution of Kenya Review Commission set up.

2002 Terrorist attacks in Mombasa kill 15 people. Opposition presidential candidate Mwai Kibaki wins landslide victory, ending Moi's 24-year rule.

2003 International Monetary Fund (IMF) resumes lending after a three-year gap.

2004 Draft of new constitution. Food crises, caused by crop failures and drought.

2005 Proposed new constitution is voted down.

2006 Countrywide drought with crop failures and livestock deaths. Corruption allegations against top ministers. Constitutional Review process restarted.

history/culture

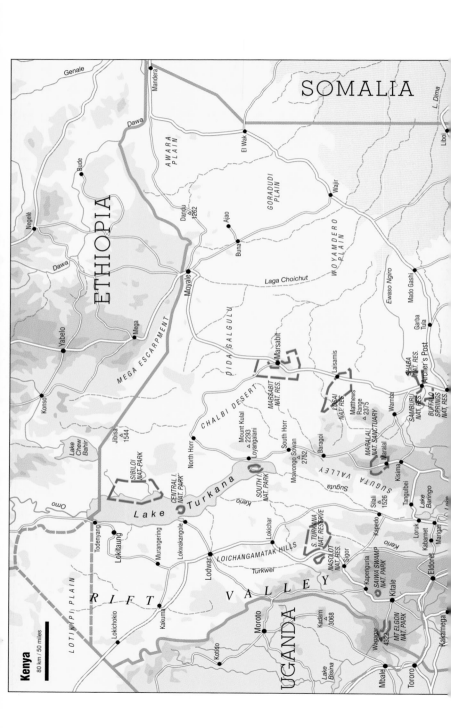

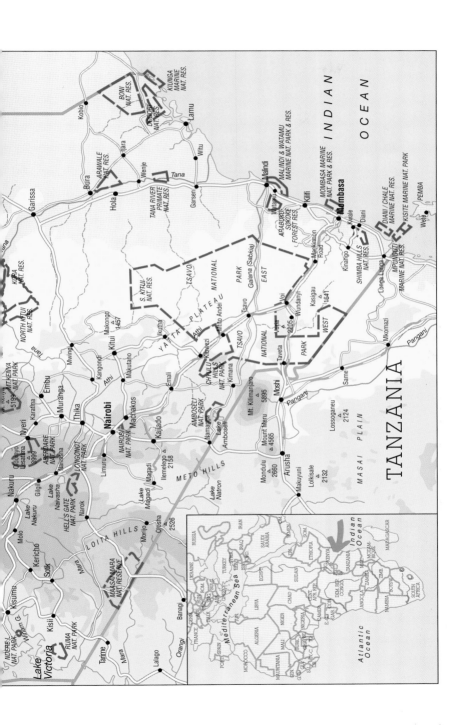

Exploring **Kenya**

Most visitors to Kenya divide their time between the game parks of the interior and the superb beaches along the coast. Reflecting this pattern, the itineraries in this book are grouped around two bases: Nairobi, well placed for the wildlife, and Mombasa, the hub of the coast. For advice on travelling between the two, *see Practical Information.*

The Nairobi section includes most of the 'safaris', with itineraries ranging from half a day to seven days. They assume the use of private transport unless otherwise specified. Inevitably, in view of the limited road network, some of the longer itineraries pass sights and attractions that are also covered in day or half-day options, so you should read and compare itineraries before setting off. If you want to take in as much as possible in seven days, we recommend the 'Grand Tour' (Itinerary 17), though this does not include the Maasai Mara.

Wildlife Checklist and Nairobi Notes

If you are interested in seeing specific wildlife, it is worth studying the Wildlife Checklist *(see pages 84–86)*, which will tell you where to go. Note: you should book accommodation in advance; details of addresses and telephone numbers are given in each itinerary.

Nairobi is pleasant but it doesn't offer much to attract the visitor. Most of the itineraries that follow therefore focus on destinations easily reached from the capital. If you want to see more of the city itself, try the following:
• A minibus tour of Nairobi and environs (book with one of the travel agencies listed on the Pocket Map).
• Visit the colourful open-air Maasai Markets selling all manner of local arts, crafts and curios. Tuesdays at the Globe Roundabout, Fridays at the Village Market on Limuru Road, and Sundays at Yaya Centre, Kilimani.
• A walk around the Arboretum (Arboretum Road, off State House Road; open daylight hours; admission free).
• On Sundays go to the races at Ngong Racecourse and see all the old colonials parading in their finery (tel: 02-566108/9).
• Visit Africa's first traditional Hindu Temple, Shree Swaminarayan Mandir on Forest Road, off Limuru Road. Admire the extensively carved stone and wooden architectural features.
• Travel on horseback from Karen out to the Lenana Forest or to the edge of the Rift Valley – full-day and half-day treks available (Nkudzi Riding School, Ngong Road, Karen; tel: 020-882512/0733-606024).
• Have lunch at the Maasai Ostrich Resort near Athi River on the Namanga Road (tel: 020-316696).
• For good 'overview' photographs or videos of Nairobi, take your camera or camcorder to Cathedral Road (near the Ministry of Health), above Uhuru Park.

Left: exceptional camera opportunity in the Maasai Mara
Right: narrow stripes and big ears identify a Grevy's zebra

itineraries from nairobi

1. IN AND AROUND NAIROBI (see map, p4)

A morning in the National Museum and Snake Park. Afternoon trip to the Safari Walk and Nairobi National Park.

From Kenyatta Avenue turn right along Uhuru Highway. At the second roundabout turn right up Museum Hill. Just before the crest of the hill turn right into the museum car park.

The **National Museum** (due to open in mid 2007 after major refurbishment; tel: 254-20-3742131, 254-20-3742161 or visit www.museums.or.ke for details) is a fascinating introduction to Kenya's eclectic culture and history. Highlights include the early man section, Joy Adamson's flower paintings or the collection of tribal artefacts in the upstairs gallery. There's also a hall of stuffed animals and a contemporary Kenyan art gallery.

The **Snake Park** is opposite the museum, on the other side of the car park, and will remain open throughout the refurbishment. Here, you can see green and black mambas, spitting cobras, pythons and other snakes from Africa and the Americas, as well as crocodile, giant tortoise, turtles and lizards, and beautiful fish in marine and freshwater aquariums. A **succulent garden** constructed next to the snake park displays indigenous succulent plants from Kenya and around East Africa. Afterwards, come out of the museum car park, turn left, down to the roundabout, and turn left on to Uhuru Highway. At the fifth roundabout turn right on to Langata Road. Drive for about 4km (2½ miles) to the turning on the left (just after Wilson Airport) to the famous **Carnivore Restaurant** (tel: 020-605933). Enjoy the All-You-Can-Eat menu of a smoking hot variety of meats cooked and served on Maasai spears and the great atmosphere.

Game Show

The game part of this day should start after lunch and last till sundown. Late afternoon and early mornings are the best times to sight game and also the best times for taking photographs, when the sun is no longer directly overhead and shadows are becoming longer.

Above: in Nairobi National Park

Leaving the Carnivore, turn left onto the Langata Road. The entrance to Nairobi National Park is a couple of kilometres along on the left. If you've opted to go to see your game in the morning, visit the park first and do the Safari Walk afterwards. If it's an afternoon excursion, visit the Safari Walk first so that you're in the National Park at sundown.

The **Safari Walk** is before the toll gate at the main entrance of the National Park, on the right (open daily 9am–6pm). Originally an animal orphanage, it is now more of a zoo, with a good collection of Kenyan inhabitants, along with a few resident exotics, such as tigers and a gorilla, given to Kenya by foreign governments, and a Wildlife Education Centre.

Nairobi National Park (open daily 6am–7pm, last admission 6.15pm; tel: 020-602121) covers 117 sq km (44 sq miles) and is fenced only on the northern and western boundaries. Consequently the game, which includes buffalo, black rhino, leopard, lion and hippos in a pool in the southeast, as well as the usual plains game (gazelles, impala, zebra, giraffe etc), is free to roam as it pleases. Ask the game scouts if there have been any sightings of particular animals that day so that you know which circuits to follow. Maps of the park are available from the shop and the snack kiosk at the entrance.

2. LIMURU AND KIAMBETHU FARM *(see map, p4)*

Half-day excursion to Limuru, with its tea plantations and the grave of Louis Leakey. Call in at Kiambethu Farm for Fiona and Marcus Vernon's talk on tea and early days in Kenya. Afterwards to the Waterfall, and then the Kentmere Club for tea.

The journey from Nairobi takes about half an hour. Phone the Vernons in advance to book your visit (tel: 066-73419/73084; email: kiambethu@ wananchi.com) and arrange to get to the farm by 11am.

From Kenyatta Avenue turn right on to Uhuru Highway. At the second roundabout turn right up Museum Hill, past the casino, on to Forest Road. At the Banana Roundabout, turn left on to the Limuru Road (C62) and drive through the valley into **Muthaiga**. Past Muthaiga's *dukas* (shops) and garage, turn left at the roundabout, keeping on the Limuru Road. Continue straight through Gigiri, past the signs for the United Nations, Village Market, Runda Estate, and on to **Ruaka** village. Turn right, following the signposts for the Kentmere Club and Waterfalls and Picnic Site. Drive through the villages of Muchatha and Banana Hill and past the Kentmere Club. Take a right into Limuru Girls' School Road.

Stop at the **All Saints' Church**, on the left a few metres after the turn-off, where the celebrated archaeologist/anthropologist, Louis Leakey, is buried. With his wife Mary, Leakey discovered the oldest-known skull of ancient man in a gorge in Tanzania, putting back the believed origins of man by about 1½ million years. It is said locally that once a year the sun shines directly through the church's rose window and casts a halo on the altar.

Right: Limuru tea-pickers, north of Nairobi

Turn left out of All Saints' churchyard on to Limuru Girls' School Road. **Kiambethu Farm** is on the left, just beyond Limuru Girls' School. The farm was built by Arnold Butler McDonnell, who arrived in Kenya at the turn of the 20th century and set up one of the first tea plantations on land he had bought for a penny an acre. His eldest daughter, Evelyn Mitchell, who died in 1999, used to welcome visitors and talk about colonial life in the old days, followed by a stroll in her few acres of indigenous forest. The tradition is carried on today by Fiona and Marcus Vernon (Mrs Mitchell's eldest daughter and son-in-law), who will show you colobus monkeys and birds, and tell you the traditional uses of many of the trees. Back at the house, ask to see Mrs Mitchell's photo

album with sepia prints of the railway station, picnics, parties and other social events in the 1920s and before. Guests are welcomed for tea at 11am, and the morning is rounded off by a four-course lunch.

Waterfalls and Tea

After lunch in the garden, drive back a few hundred metres along Limuru Girls' School Road and turn left at the signs to visit the **Waterfall**. This is a short but quite steep stroll from the picnic site, and is best avoided on Sundays when many Nairobi residents drive up from the city to spend the afternoon here. I suggest you then go on to the **Kentmere Club** for tea and to check out the gardens and the amazing menu. To return to Nairobi, turn left out of the Kentmere, then take the first turn on the right. This road winds down through the valley, past slopes planted with coffee, and a saw-mill. At the T-junction turn left on to the (C62) Limuru Road and drive back, through Ruaka, past Village Market Shopping Centre and Muthaiga, into town.

3. OUT OF AFRICA *(see map, p4)*

A full-day excursion taking in Daphne Sheldrick's animal orphanage, the Giraffe Centre, the Karen Blixen Museum, lunch in Karen and an afternoon at the Bomas of Kenya.

From Kenyatta Avenue turn left on to Uhuru Highway. At the third roundabout turn right on to Langata Road. Drive past the army barracks and Nairobi National Park to the Magadi Road and turn left, past Brookhouse School and Banda School, then past Mukoma Road and down a steep hill. At the bottom on the left is the Mbagathi Gate entrance to Nairobi National Park and the **David Sheldrick Wildlife Trust**. Sheldrick was the founder-warden of Tsavo National Park, and here his widow Daphne cares for orphaned elephants and rhinos. The orphanage is open daily 11am–noon, when you can watch the orphans being fed (tel: 020-891996).

On leaving the orphanage, retrace your route to the main road and turn right on to Magadi Road. When you reach the Langata Road, turn left and drive

Above: snacks for two of the residents of the Giraffe Centre
Right: traditional dancing at the Bomas of Kenya

to the junction of Langata South Road. Turn left here and follow the signs to the Giraffe Centre/African Fund for Endangered Wildlife (AFEW), off Koitobus Road. En route, the **Matbronze Wildlife Art Gallery** (on Kifaru Land, just off Langata South Road before the road to the Giraffe Centre) displays wildlife sculptures cast in the 'lost-wax' method. Also off Langata South Road, on Bogani East Road, is the **Utamaduni Craft Centre**, a country house with a number of small shops selling local curios and handicrafts.

The **Giraffe Centre** (tel: 020-891658 or 890952; open daily 9.30am–5.30pm) was set up to save the endangered Rothschild or Ugandan giraffe, whose natural habitat in Northern Uganda/Southern Sudan was being threatened by agriculture. It's great fun to feed the giraffes with horse nuts provided by the warden from a raised platform that puts you on a level with their heads and astonishing long tongues. Have morning coffee here.

Blixen Museum

Afterwards drive back to Langata Road and turn left. Continue as far as Karen Road left. Turn left here and drive for about 2½km (1½ miles) to reach the **Karen Blixen Museum** (tel: 020-882779; open daily, 9.30am–6pm). Although this is the house where she lived and which is described in *Out of Africa*, not much remains of Blixen's original possessions (most of them were sold when she left Kenya in 1931 and some are in the MacMillan Library in Nairobi). But Universal Pictures donated some of the props used in making the film, and these are on display.

Turn left out of the museum on to Karen Road, then left at the crossroads on to Langata Road and drive for 1½km (1 mile). Park at the *duka* (grocery store) on the left before the roundabout. Before lunch look at the beautifully made handicrafts (candelabras, wooden picture frames, hand-blown glass, leatherwork, wrought iron etc) in Marco Polo and Siafu shops. Lunch options in Karen include the **Horseman** in the Shopping Centre, the **Talisman** on Ngong Road (turn left at the roundabout) or the **Rusty Nail** on Dagoretti Road (straight on at the roundabout).

After lunch drive back along Langata Road towards Nairobi. Go past Langata South Road and turn left into Forest Edge Road for the **Bomas of Kenya** cultural centre. If you can, arrive by 2pm – it's less than 15 minutes from Karen. Watch their display of traditional dancing, visit the huts and see the handicrafts of some of Kenya's principal ethnic groups. To return to Nairobi, drive back to Langata Road and turn left.

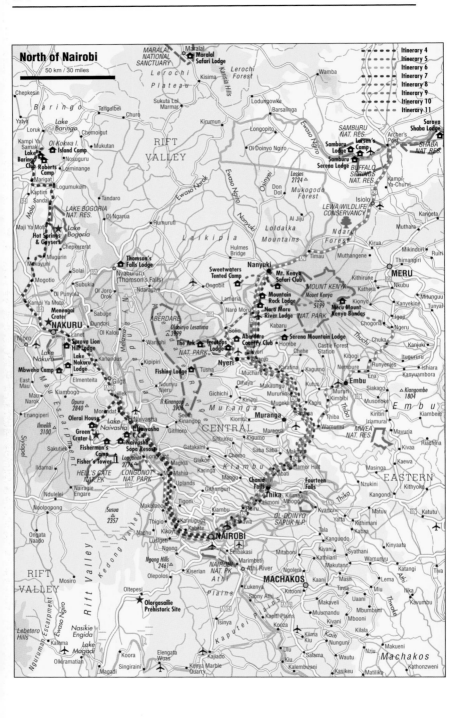

4. LAKE NAIVASHA *(see map, p26)*

An overnight trip to Lake Naivasha, with beautiful views over the Rift Valley, and Crater Lake Sanctuary with its teeming wildlife. Dinner in an Art Deco house (black tie optional).

Set off early to arrive in Naivasha mid-morning. To begin with, follow Itinerary 5 *(see page 28)* but don't turn off the dual carriageway for Longonot. Drive past the first viewpoint over the Rift Valley at 2,440m (8,000ft) – it's signposted – and stop at the second, which has a petrol station at the exit to the viewpoint. You get a much better view from here and you won't be so hassled by souvenir sellers. At this point the land drops down to the valley floor with breathtaking views of mounts **Longonot** and **Susua** and **Lake Naivasha**. (See Itinerary 5 for directions on climbing Mount Longonot.)

From here, the road steeply descends to Lake Naivasha, still 45 minutes away. Drive past two exits to Naivasha town on your left and continue for another 10km (6 miles) to the Moi North Lake Road. Turn left here on to a dirt road and drive 19km (12 miles) to **Olerai House** (tel: 020-891112/890596; email: oleraihouse@africaonline.co.ke; www.elephantwatchsafaris.com). This is where you will spend the night.

Olerai was the childhood home of Oria Douglas-Hamilton, who, with her husband Iain, is well known for conservation work, particularly with elephants. After lunch in the garden, enjoy a romantic cruise along the lake's edge in the African Gondola, or spend the afternoon by the pool in the beautiful garden with a good book from the library, before changing for a sumptuous dinner on the terrace.

Next morning, wander through the private game sanctuary with plains and woodlands that have colobus monkeys, zebra, numerous antelopes including Thomson's gazelle and waterbuck, and many birds. En route visit Sirocco House, now the Douglas-Hamilton family home (built in the 1930s, it is a fine example of Art

Above: cliffs in Hell's Gate National Park
Right: a black-and-white colobus

Deco architecture), before choosing one of the options listed below. You can drive back to Nairobi in the afternoon.

Make Your Choice
Options for the second day:
• Sailing, boating, waterskiing, wind-surfing, birdwatching and fishing can all be arranged at Olerai House.

• Play 18 holes of golf with stunning views over Lake Naivasha at The Great Rift Valley Lodge & Golf Resort (tel: 050-50048; email: rvgolf@heritage hotels.co.ke).

• Take a scenic flight over the Great Rift Valley, taking in Lakes Naivasha, El-emeteita, Nakuru and the volcanic mountains of Suswa, Longonot, Eburru and Menengai (tel: 050-50050/4015443; email: jillangus@africaonline.co.ke).

• **Elsamere Conservation Centre** near Crescent Island (on Moi South Lake Road): watch a film on the life of the late Joy Adamson who raised Elsa, the orphan lion cub made famous in the book and film *Born Free*. Have tea on the lawn of her home (daily 3–6pm). All proceeds go towards wildlife conservation. To contact the centre in advance, tel: 050-2021055/74, or write to PO Box 1497, Naivasha.

• **Hell's Gate National Park**, named after its steaming hot springs, contains East Africa's largest geothermal plant and is one of the few parks in which you are free to walk or cycle. There is plenty of game to see, including lions and leopards. The entrance is well signposted, off Moi South Lake Road.

• **Elmenteita Weavers**: watch cotton and wool fabrics being hand-woven and buy carved wooden birds, ceramics, cushions, bedspreads, tablecloths, napkins etc. Find them on Moi South Lake Road, on the right about 200m (220 yards) after the turn-off for Lake Naivasha Country Club.

5. TO THE TOP OF A VOLCANO *(see map, p26)*
A morning excursion to Mount Longonot, including a climb to the volcano's top, views of the Rift Valley and lunch in Naivasha.

Head north out of Nairobi on Uhuru Highway, stopping at the ABC Shopping Centre on the left to buy something to drink and some snacks (such as fruit and chocolate) to eat on the top of Longonot. Continue out of town along Waiyaki Way (A104). You'll see crafts and produce for sale on the side of the roads – sheepskin hats, wicker baskets, fruit and vegetables, soapstone carvings, live fish, etc. Turn left at the end of the dual carriageway, shortly after the viewpoint signposted at 2,440m (8,000ft), following the signs to **Longonot**. Just before the road crosses the railway, there's a signpost on

Above: you can climb to the top of Mount Longonot
Right: hippos take it easy in Lake Nakuru

the left to Mt Longonot National Park. The park entrance and parking area is 6 km (4 miles) along this dirt road.

It takes about 2 hours to climb to the summit of Longonot, known to the Maasai as *Oloonong'ot* (steep-ridged mountain). At 2,776m (9,108ft), it is the highest Rift Valley volcano in Kenya. It takes another 3 hours to walk around the rim (in either direction). Be careful because the path crumbles in places and there's a steep drop. Buffalo are said to live in the vegetation at the bottom of the crater, though how they got there, nobody knows.

Walk back down the mountain, drive back to the main road and turn left towards Naivasha. Drive towards Lake Naivasha for about 17km (11 miles), turn left down Moi South Lake Road towards Hell's Gate National Park. After a couple of kilometres, you will see a signpost on your right for **Lake Naivasha Country Club** (tel: 050-2021160/202095; www.blockhotelske.com). Further on are **Lake Naivasha Simba Lodge** (tel: 050-50305/6/7) and **Lake Naivasha Sopa Resort** (tel: 020-3750183; www.sopalodges.com). These are all beautiful spots to have lunch or to hire a boat to go birdwatching.

Afterwards, you can take the A104 straight back to Nairobi.

6. LAKE NAKURU NATIONAL PARK *(see map, p26)*

An overnight trip to see the wildlife of Lake Nakuru National Park.

Though this itinerary is designed as an overnight excursion, it would also make an enjoyable day-trip from Nairobi.

Follow Itineraries 4 and 5 on the Uhuru Highway, along Waiyaki Way (A104) past Longonot to Naivasha but, instead of taking the turn-off to Naivasha town, continue straight along on the A104. Nakuru is over an hour's drive (67km/ 42 miles) further north on very rough tarmac. You'll pass Gilgil and Lake Elmenteita before arriving in Nakuru, which in Maasai means 'dust bowl'.

Lake Nakuru is famous for its flamingos which from a distance appear like pink icing over the lake. There are also pelicans, storks and numerous other bird species, as well as lion, leopard, bushbuck, waterbuck, impala, gazelles, rhino, monkeys, baboons and hippo (best seen at sunset when they

itineraries from nairobi

yawn, snort and climb out of the mud on to the shore to graze). There are also more than 120 Rothschild's giraffes in the park.

This is a well-maintained and easily accessible game park, with roads in good condition and suitable for even two-wheel-drive vehicles. It takes around 2 hours to drive around the lake. Don't miss the euphorbia (candelabra trees) on the west side, the largest euphorbia forest in East Africa. You may spot black rhino in the grasslands in the south and white rhino in the southeast.

Drive down towards the lake shore (mud and season permitting) but don't go too close or you might get stuck. Stop about 35m (40 yds) from the water and get out of your vehicle for a closer look at the birds. Then drive up to **Baboon Cliffs** for a view over the lake, which is particularly impressive when a storm is rolling up the Rift Valley. But watch that storm closely!

Stay the night at **Sarova Lion Hill** (tel: 051-850235/288; www.sarova hotels.com) or at **Lake Nakuru Lodge** (tel: 051-850228; www.lakenakuru lodge.com). Next day, it's worth getting up early to go on a game drive before breakfast. You'll be able to watch birds waking up, preening and feeding, and see the hippos returning to the water after their night's grazing. Set off back to Nairobi in the early afternoon, aiming to arrive in the city before dusk.

7. LUXURY IN NANYUKI *(see map, p26)*

An overnight trip to Nanyuki and Mount Kenya Safari Club, waking early on the second day to take a pre-dawn horse-back ride through Mount Kenya Game Ranch.

Mount Kenya Safari Club is 205km (127 miles) or about 3 hours from Nairobi and makes a very relaxing overnight excursion. It can also be combined with a trip to The Ark (Itinerary 8) and with trips further north to Isiolo and Samburu (Itinerary 9), Lewa Wildlife Conservancy (Itinerary 16) or Maralal and Turkana (Itinerary 17).

From Moi Avenue in Nairobi take Muranga Road down to the big roundabout, go straight ahead up the hill, bear right, and stay on Muranga Road until the Muthaiga roundabout. Take the third exit and follow signs for the A2 to Thika, going straight over the next two roundabouts. This road bypasses Kahawa Army barracks, Thika town, and goes through Karatina, 128km (80 miles) from Nairobi. It is good tarmac all the way, although occasional potholes do appear unexpectedly, so drive with care.

This very fertile region is settled with predominantly Kikuyu smallholdings and was the heartland of the *Mau Mau* rebellion that eventually led to Kenyan independence *(see History & Culture)*.

The turn-off to the right for **Nanyuki** is at the bottom of a curving hill, 13km (8 miles) after Karatina, and is clearly signposted to the Aberdare Country Club, Naro Moru River Lodge and Mountain Lodge.

Mount Kenya Safari Club (tel: 062-30000 or 020-216940; www.lonrho hotels.com) is also well signposted and is 64km (40 miles) from this turn-off.

Above: cross the Equator just south of Nanyuki town

Just after the equator crossing, the turning to the Club is on the right just before Nanyuki town.

The opulent Safari Club was established by a Texan oil baron, a Swiss millionaire and film star William Holden. After checking in, book tomorrow's pre-breakfast horse ride at the reception and then wander (or jog) around the 36 hectares (90 acres) of beautifully manicured gardens, complete with sacred ibis, yellow-billed storks, Egyptian geese, peacocks, ornamental ponds and superb views of snow-capped Mount Kenya; or swim in the only heated swimming-pool on the equator. You can also play golf, tennis, bowls, croquet or snooker, go fishing, birdwatching or mountain-climbing, or use the health and beauty centre. There's also an art gallery selling some magnificent (but expensive) works.

After lunch, visit the **animal orphanage** to see Kenya's only captive breeding herd of bongo. Other animals include monkeys, cheetah, gazelles, zebra and other orphaned or wounded animals that need medical care before they can be rehabilitated to life in the wild. Relax before dressing for the seven-course dinner – this is one of the few Kenyan restaurants where men are required to wear a jacket and tie (women should also dress smartly).

On Horseback

Next morning, ride before breakfast. On horseback is the best way to approach most African game, because the latter cannot smell you or recognise your silhouette as that of a human when you are in the saddle. Ask to explore the 485 hectares (1,200 acres) of bushland that have been transformed into Mount Kenya Game Ranch (not actually part of the Safari Club, but the staff should be able to request access for you). Or book a morning game drive to Ol Pejeta Conservancy, including a visit to the Chimp and Rhino Sancturies. Or arrange a scenic aerial flight over Mt Kenya and Laikipia (Tropic Air Ltd; tel: 062-32890/1; www.tropicairkenya.com).

Before setting off back to Nairobi, you can visit **Nanyuki Spinners and Weavers** (tel: 062-32062/31724; open Mon–Fri 9am–5pm, Sat 9am–1pm). This women's cooperative makes beautiful hand-spun, hand-woven rugs, shawls and blankets coloured with locally produced natural plant dyes. To watch the women at work, drive back to the A2, turn right and drive through Nanyuki town. Turn left on to the C76 (Laikipia Road) at Kenya Commercial Bank. The workshops are 1km (½ mile) along this road on the left opposite the District Hospital.

Just after leaving Nanyuki to return to Nairobi, stop off at Nanyuki Airfield for lunch at Barney's Restaurant, or at the Trout Tree Restaurant – built in a big beautiful Mugumo tree overlooking the trout hatchery (3km/2 miles further on).

Above: relax at Mount Kenya Safari Club
Right: at the Safari Club's animal orphanage

8. ABERDARE NATIONAL PARK *(see map, p26)*

A two-night trip to Aberdare National Park, a region famous for its lions, and Sweetwaters Tented Camp, with log fires, floodlit water-holes, waterfalls and flame trees.

Follow Itinerary 7 as far as Karatina. Don't take the turn-off for Nanyuki – in spite of the sign saying Aberdare Country Club. Instead, continue straight ahead and into Nyeri town. Drive through Nyeri town towards Mweiga. Follow the signs to the Aberdare Country Club up a dirt road on the right.

The **Aberdare Country Club** (tel: 061-55620 or 020-216940; www.lonrhohotels.com) was at one time a watering-hole for early white settlers and is now a luxurious lodge/hotel with a nine-hole golf course, riding, fishing, tennis, views of Mount Kenya and a wildlife sanctuary to walk in. It's a popular overnight weekend haunt for the expatriate community.

The **Aberdares** are a steep volcanic massif covered in moorland and dense forest (with some of the oldest trees in the country) to the west of Mount Kenya. This beautiful but wild region is home to some of the fiercest lions in Kenya and great care should be taken when lions are sighted. Black leopard and other melanistic (dark-coloured) animals, including serval cats, also live here. There is excellent trout-fishing in the high mountain streams and impressive waterfalls.

Aberdare National Park is not easy to visit because the dirt roads are inaccessible in heavy rains (and it rains a lot) and the thick forest makes game viewing difficult. However, a good place to stay is **The Ark**, managed by Fairmount Hotels & Resorts (www.lonrhohotels.com) and built like Noah's vessel in a sea of trees. (Transport is provided from the Aberdare Country Club to The Ark, leaving at 2.30pm and arriving about 45 minutes later after a short drive through the game park.) The floodlit salt lick and waterhole attract

elephant, rhino, lion, gazelle, leopard, antelope and other animals, particularly after dark.

Watch from the comfort of the glass-walled bar with its roaring log fire (it gets very cold at night) or go down into the lookout hide close to the waterhole. This has open window slits so that you can not only see every whisker but also smell the elephant and buffalo a few metres away. The resident game warden (yes, they call him Noah) keeps watch at night and will wake you if he sights anything unusual in the small hours. Children under seven years old are not allowed to stay here. Stay overnight at The Ark, returning to Aberdare Country Club for lunch next day. Arrange to visit **Solio Game Ranch** after breakfast next day (tel: Nairobi

Left: lionesses come to drink at The Ark's waterhole

020-240157; PO Box 30595, 00100 Nairobi; email: eparfet@africaonline. co.ke; or via Aberdare Country Club, which has a special arrangement with Solio). This private ranch set in thorn-scrub and open grassland is now a rhino sanctuary and has been successful in reintroducing rhinos to the wild. You may also see oryx, eland, leopard, giraffe and colobus monkeys. To get there, take the road to Nyahururu from the Aberdare Country Club. Drive for about 8km (5 miles) and turn right at the signs for Solio Ranch, just after the big dip.

Tents with a View

Just north of the equator is **Sweetwaters Tented Camp** (tel: 062-32409; or through Serena Hotels, Nairobi, tel: 020-2711077/8; www.serenahotels.com), a few kilometres outside **Nanyuki**. Turn left out of the Aberdare Country Club and follow the dirt road to the main tarmac road. Turn left towards Nanyuki. The turn-off for Sweetwaters is 1km (½ mile) before town on the left, opposite the old Silverbeck Hotel, just after the equator. It's 15km (9 miles) from here.

The land used to belong to Adnan Kashoggi, the arms dealer, but was taken over by Lonrho in settlement of debts. The luxurious safari tents (with bathrooms) have incredible views of Mount Kenya and overlook a waterhole frequented by elephants and other game. You can take game drives round the ranch at sunrise and sundown. Be sure to visit the rhino and chimpanzee sanctuaries.

Return to Nairobi via Kiganjo and **Thika**, allowing 3 hours to reach the capital before nightfall. Stop off at the Blue Posts Inn just before Thika to visit the waterfalls and admire the colourful trees made famous in Elspeth Huxley's novel *The Flame Trees of Thika*.

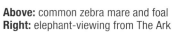

Above: common zebra mare and foal
Right: elephant-viewing from The Ark

itineraries from nairobi

9. SAMBURU AND SHABA *(see map, p26)*

A two-night excursion to the northern game country, stopping en route to see traditional craftsmen at work. Stay the first night in Samburu, rising early to explore Buffalo Springs, and the second night at Shaba.

The region that used to be called the Northern Frontier District is a stark, rugged landscape where nomads still drive their herds chasing the ephemeral growth of grass. It is the emptiness and wildness that makes a visit to the Samburu, Buffalo Springs and Shaba National Reserves such an unforgettable experience. If you leave Nairobi by 8.30am you will be in Samburu by lunchtime. Follow Itinerary 7 as far as Nanyuki. Drive straight through town and continue along the A2 through Timau to Isiolo – it's about 300km (185 miles) or 4 hours on fairly good tarmac roads from the capital. A four-wheel-drive vehicle is recommended for this trip.

People Watching

Isiolo is the frontier town bordering the wilds of northern Kenya. A crossroads for Samburu, Somalis, Rendille, Boran and Turkana peoples, it's a great place to people-watch. In the colourful market, on the left as you enter town, local youths sell souvenirs including beaten steel, copper and brass bangles, and Somali daggers in intricately decorated leather sheaths. These vendors can be very persistent, so be polite but firm or you'll find yourself loaded with trinkets you don't really want. For a few shillings, they will take you behind the market to see the craftsmen at work, huddled over outdoor fires heated white-hot with foot-pumped bellows made from a goat's stomach, or hammering the hot metal on improvised anvils.

Before leaving Isiolo, fill up with petrol at one of the garages about 300m (325 yds) further down the A2 into town. Then keep straight on (drive slowly through town as the road is very rough) until you get to the police check-point where you must register your vehicle. Continue north, bearing left on the main road 100 metres after the barrier. Beyond this point the terrain is very

Above: rear view of Grevy's zebra drinking

wild and barren, and very dusty in the dry season. You're now on the main road to Samburu, Buffalo Springs and Shaba National Reserves, about 45km (28 miles) away. The dirt roads from Isiolo are heavily corrugated, and can be rough and bouncy. Inside the reserves, the roads are usually smoother (although still dirt) and the wildlife makes up for any discomfort.

Cross over the Ewaso Ngiro River, drive into Archer's Post village where you turn left to enter **Samburu** by the Archer's Post Gate. (Before you do, you might visit the **Uaso Cultural Centre**, a women's self-help community-based group, 1km/½ mile from Archer's Post: it's open daily 6am–6pm). Inside the reserve, make for **Larsen's Camp** (tel: 064-31373/4 or 020-532329/650392; www.wildernesslodges.co.ke), where you're staying the night – the ultimate in luxury tented camps. On the way, look out for blue-legged Somali ostrich, Grevy's zebra, leopard, elephant, reticulated giraffe, oryx and cheetah. Birds are abundant, with more than 365 species recorded.

After a late lunch, a siesta and tea, take a game drive west along the river. Drive back to Samburu Lodge in time for the leopard-baiting at sundown and to see the crocodiles feed. It's close to Larsen's Camp so you can drive back there before dark. Alternative accommodation in Samburu: **Samburu Lodge** (contact Wilderness Lodges, as above); **Samburu Serena Safari Lodge** (tel: 020-2711077/8; www.serenahotels.com); **Samburu Intrepids** (tel: 064-30813 or 020-4447929/4446651; www.heritage-eastafrica.com); or the luxurious **Elephant Watch Camp** (tel: 020-891112; www.elephantwatchsafaris.com).

Copper-coloured Hills

Before breakfast next day, cross over the river and take a game drive in **Buffalo Springs National Reserve**, which adjoins Samburu. Follow the road east along the river to get to the **Buffalo Springs** (which were apparently blasted out of the ground when an Italian pilot dumped his bombs in the reserve during World War II). Exit Samburu by the Buffalo Springs Gate and turn left on to the A2 to Marsabit. Drive a little way north, towards Archer's Post and then turn right at the signposts for Sarova Shaba Lodge.

Like Samburu, **Shaba National Reserve** is on the banks of the Ewaso Ngiro ('Brown River'). More remote and less visited than Samburu, this is the reserve where the late Joy Adamson reha-bilitated leopards to the wild. It takes its name from Mount Shaba, a copper-coloured sand-stone hill. A series of springs bubble up in the river on the northeastern side of the reserve. One spring, Penny's Drop, was named after Joy Adamson's leopard Penny, which she re-leased back into the wild in Shaba Reserve.

Stay the night at **Sarova Shaba Lodge** (tel: 020-2713333 or 064-30638; www.sarova hotels.com) or stay at the small luxury tented camp, **Joy's Camp** (tel: 020-603090; www. chelipeacock.com), overlooking a natural spring. Leave Shaba by 2pm at the latest next day to get back to Nairobi by nightfall.

Right: the nomadic Samburu live mainly in northern Kenya

10. THREE LAKES *(see map, p26)*

A three-day trip to Lake Nakuru (flamingos and pelicans), Lake Bogoria (hot springs and geysers) and Lake Baringo (hippos, crocodiles, bird walks and boating).

You'll be driving on both tarmac and some quite rough dirt roads, so a four-wheel-drive vehicle is essential for this itinerary. Note: my recommended overnight accommodation, Lake Baringo Island Camp, rises steeply out of the water and there are no fences, so if you take young children, they should be supervised at all times.

On day one of this tour, follow Itinerary 6 to Lake Nakuru, staying at **Sarova Lion Hill** (tel: 051-850236/020-2713333; www.sarovahotels.com). Before going to sleep, order a picnic lunch box for the next day. In the morning, take a game drive in the park before breakfast, then drive back through the main park gate along Flamingo and Moi roads to Nakuru town. Turn left on to Kenyatta Avenue and follow signs for the B4, signposted to Marigat. Pass through Kampi ya Moto and turn right at Mogotio on to the dirt road signposted to **Lake Bogoria National Reserve**.

Flamingos Galore

Bogoria is a shallow soda lake at the foot of the sheer-faced Laikipia Escarpment. The landscape is burnt and rocky and seemingly inhospitable to wildlife. However, there are sometimes more flamingos here than at Lake Nakuru further south, though this depends on the depth of water and the amount of algae it contains. There are also hundreds of other birds and some game, including the usual gazelle, impala etc.

You are taking a back route to the lake but apart from a few stony patches, the road is well graded. On leaving Mogotio, for the next 24km (15 miles) you drive alongside spiky sisal plantations as far as Mugurin. Drive straight on for 20km (12 miles) from Mugurin and turn right at Maji ya Moto to enter the reserve by the western Majimoto Gate. Drive down towards the lake and take the left fork to get to the **hot springs**. Here, you can get out and walk down to the water's edge to watch the geysers – but be careful: many visitors have been burned by the hot jets.

On leaving the hot springs turn left and drive to the southern end of the park.

Look out for klipspringers and greater kudu here. Retrace your route past the hot springs and exit the reserve by the northern Loboi Gate. Before leaving, follow the smaller tracks down to the flat lake bed, turn off your engine and get out and walk around. It's the best way to appreciate the silence and heat.

If you're tempted to tarry a while, there's accommodation nearby at **Lake Bogoria Hotel** (tel: 051-2216441 or 020-249055; www.bogoriasparesort.com), which has the only naturally heated spa in Kenya.

Once out of the reserve, drive 21km (13 miles) along the E461 dirt road to the tarmacked B4 road from Nakuru to Loruk. Turn right (this junction is signposted) and continue through Marigat to the junction on the right leading to **Kampi ya Samaki**, 123km (76 miles) from Nakuru. There's a garage on the corner. Drive another 3km (2 miles), past **Lake Baringo Club** (tel: 053-51401 or 020-4450639; keen birders should call in to arrange a bird walk along the cliffs for the following afternoon) and follow the dirt road through Kampi ya Samaki village (ask for directions if you can't find the signposts to Island Camp). Drive to the end then follow the track down to the lake. Park your car here, remembering to take all valuables with you, then walk down to the jetty and wait to be whisked across the water in a dinghy on the 20-minute trip to **Lake Baringo Island Camp** on Ol Kokwa Island (tel: 051-850858 or 020-884216; www.island-camp.com).

Crocodiles, Hippos and More

The freshwater Lake Baringo is one of the most northern of the Rift Valley lakes and is home to crocodiles, hippos and more than 450 species of birds. The water looks muddy due to its chemical composition which keeps silt particles circulating and stops them sinking to the bottom. Just before dawn, the lake is quite still, but when a storm rolls over the valley, the water churns with waves several metres high. Although crocodiles come quite close to the island, it's possible to swim or ski in the lake, as advised by the camp staff.

On Ol Kokwa Island you can swim in the pool, sit and watch the lake or take a guided bird walk. The luxury tents have their own bird feeder and great views. To unwind fully, stay here two nights. There's a beautiful pre-breakfast boat trip up the **Molo River** – with hippo and numerous water birds en route – but it's only possible in the wet season, and then only for the adventurous. Arrange to see the village of the local Njemps people.

Return to Nairobi via Nakuru and Naivasha – even with a pause for sodas the city is just over 4 hours away.

Left: a lone hippo in Lake Baringo at sunset
Above: a successful fishing trip on Lake Baringo

11. MOUNT KENYA *(see map, p26)*

A five-day trek from east to west across Mount Kenya.

Camping stoves, boots, waterproofs, tents, balaclavas, torches etc can be hired from Alliance Naro Moru River Lodge (tel: 062-62212/62201 or 020-4443357/8; www.alliancehotels.com/naromoru.htm). Alternatively, book your climb with Let's Go Travel, tel: 020-4447151/4441030; www.lets-go-travel.net. They will organise your itinerary, porters, transport and equipment.

You don't have to be a mountaineer to cross Mount Kenya (5,199m/17,057ft) but it's a stiff walk and you need to be properly equipped and fit. Ideally, you should have experienced climbing at this height before, to know how your body will react, and you should certainly do some sort of training (such as serious walking) before you attempt the climb.

Don't even think of climbing without a warm sleeping-bag, warm clothes, including gloves, scarf and hat, and walking boots. The clouds roll down from the mountaintop around lunchtime, and it rains or snows almost every day, even in the dry season. You can request guides and porters to carry your equipment (contact Naro Moru River Lodge or Let's Go Travel, as above) and remember to take your own food as there are no shops or restaurants en route or have this included when you book the climb.

The most beautiful route takes you up from Chogoria village to the west, around the peaks to the south, then down via the short Naro Moru route. On the way, watch your step, but also look out for buffalo, elephant, malachite sunbirds, eagles, rock hyrax, giant lobelia, groundsel and alpine heather.

On the Right Track

To get to the starting-point, follow Itinerary 7 as far as Thika. Continue on the A2, then take the turn-off for Embu and Meru (the B6), 86km (53

miles) from Nairobi. Drive through Embu town and the villages of Runyenjes and Marima. Take the signposted left turn-off to Kiangoji (D474), 3km (2 miles) after Marima. Drive for 3km (2 miles) past the Chogoria Transit Hotel and turn left at the Mukutano Bar and Restaurant. Drive for 4km (2½ miles) past the shops and turn right. Chogoria Forest Station is about 1km (½ mile) down this road.

The park entrance is 21km (13 miles) further up at 2,990m (9,810ft). The road passes through mountain forest and, in a series of hairpin bends, steep hills up to the bamboo zone. Spend the night at **Meru Mount Kenya Bandas** (take the right turn-off just before the gate entrance on the right). This is where your guide and/or porters will meet you before the

Left: Shipton's Notch, on the West Ridge, seen from the Batian summit

Mountain Sickness

More people die of pulmonary oedema on Mount Kenya each year than on any other mountain. It is caused by an accumulation of water on the lungs. The symptoms are headaches, nausea, sleeplessness, loss of appetite, swelling and fluid retention, breathing difficulties, slurred speech and abnormal behaviour. The only cure is to get to a lower altitude – as quickly as possible. To avoid pulmonary oedema, allow time to get accustomed to the altitude before going higher up.

climb. Ask to stay in the cottage when you book (Let's Go Travel, as above).

If you have a driver, ask him to pick you up at the Naro Moru park entrance in four days' time. If you don't have a driver, you may be able to arrange for transport back to your car with Naro Moru River Lodge or Let's Go Travel. Either way, your return trip should be arranged and confirmed before you set off.

Set out early next morning on the 5-hour walk to **Minto's Hut** where you will camp. The path crosses a stream and then follows the ridge and is well marked. The views down to the Gorges Valley are superb. Remember to take water with you as there are no fresh sources en route.

To Point Lenana

On the third day walk to the **Austrian Hut**, at the foot of Point Lenana. The route leads up the valley, across scree slopes, and (very steeply) up to Square Tarn. From here, continue straight on to the col below Point Lenana, descend for a short way, then continue over another scree slope to the Austrian Hut. You should spend the night here.

Another early start the next morning: set off at 4.30am to climb to **Point Lenana**, a steep 1½-hour scramble. There's only one way, so you can't get lost. Take only chocolate and water with you – leave the rest of your baggage with the porters. You'll be at the top of the mountain at dawn when the views are clearest and you'll feel justly proud of yourself and exhilarated that you've climbed the second highest mountain in Africa. Come down to breakfast at Austrian Hut and then descend the steep scree slope to **Mackinders Hut** on the west side of the mountain, about 1½ hours away. Spend the day pottering around and relaxing here.

Next morning, walk down through the steeply sloping bog – set at a 45-degree angle and streaming with rivulets of water all through the year – across open moorland and down through the forest to the Meteorological Station road head. From here it's only 9km (5 miles) to the park gate where your driver should be waiting to take you to Naro Moru River Lodge for refreshments and a celebratory drink. (If you set off early, you can walk from Lenana to Naro Moru in one day, although by the end your knees will be trembling.)

You can easily drive back to Nairobi the same day. From Naro Moru River Lodge drive back to the main A2 road and turn right. Nairobi is 171km (106 miles) or about 2¼ hours away.

Right: camping at over 4,000 metres (13,000 ft) on Mount Kenya

12. AMBOSELI NATIONAL PARK *(see map below)*

An overnight trip to see the wildlife of Amboseli National Park, against the backdrop of Africa's highest peak.

If you don't want to drive to Amboseli, you can fly from Wilson Airport in Nairobi or from Mombasa (see Practical Information, page 87).

Take Uhuru Highway south out of central Nairobi and drive straight on, continuing on the Mombasa road. After 24km (15 miles) you reach Athi River, where you turn right on to the A104, heading through Isinya and Kajiado for Namanga and the Tanzanian border, 135km (85 miles) away. On a clear day, you'll see Kilimanjaro, at 5,895m (19,340ft) the highest peak in Africa, for most of the journey.

In Namanga town, just before the border post, turn left by a petrol station and follow the signs to the C103. The entrance to the Amboseli National Park is 70km (43 miles) further on. This dirt road is heavily corrugated and usually has some washaways, so you might find the drive rather tiring. As you continue through the park you'll see the shimmering mirage of the dry **Lake Amboseli** (Maasai for 'salt dust') which fills up with

Above: Amboseli has no shortage of elephants

water only very occasionally in the rainy season. You'll also see plenty of dead trees, killed by volcanic salts in the underground water and by foraging elephants (there are hundreds of them in the freshwater swamps to the southeast). Tourist vehicles driving off-road are also partly responsible for the destruction, so stick to the tracks, no matter how tempted you are to get close to the wildlife.

Don't be put off by first impressions – Amboseli's charm will soon win you over. Be sure to watch the sun set behind Kilimanjaro and look out for Maasai *morani* (warriors) watering their cattle: be prepared to pay them if you want to take their pictures. You'll also see buffalo, gazelle, hyena, giraffe, baboon, vultures, plenty of flamingos and maybe even rhino and lion.

You should book to stay the night at the **Amboseli Serena Lodge** (tel: 045) 622361; www.serenahotels.com) or at **Ol Tukai Lodge** (tel: 020-4445514; www.oltukailodge.com). Or stay at **Tortilis**, a luxury tented lodge situated on the southern border of the park (tel: 020-603090; www.chelipeacock.com). Then return to Nairobi the next day, leaving by lunchtime at the latest.

13. LAKE MAGADI *(see map, p40)*

A day trip to see the birdlife of Lake Magadi, with views of the Ngong Hills and Rift Valley and a visit to Olorgasailie prehistoric site en route, with the option of continuing west for two nights' stay on the edge of the Nguruman Escarpment overlooking the Great Rift Valley.

This is one of the hottest, least populated places in Kenya, so take plenty of water, something to eat and extra fuel. Be sure to travel only in a reliable vehicle. A four-wheel-drive vehicle is essential if you plan to travel beyond Magadi.

The day before you set off, order your picnic lunch from Pasara Café and Bar (Ground Floor, Lonrho House on Standard/Kaunda Street; tel: 020-241247/343696). From Kenyatta Avenue, turn left along Uhuru Highway to the third roundabout. Turn right on to Langata Road and drive out past Nairobi National Park to Magadi Road (C58). Turn left here and drive on through Ongata Rongai, and up the southeast flank of the Ngong Hills at 2,135m (7,005ft).

About 32km (20 miles) from Nairobi, the road drops dramatically to the Rift Valley floor below. When you reach the shoulder of the Ngong Hills, before you drive down the west side, follow the dirt road on the left to the viewpoint. This is the vista that is said to have inspired Karen Blixen to write *Out of Africa*.

Follow the C58 down the hairpin bends of the escarpment. Just

Right: on the road from the Ngong Hills to Lake Magadi

after tiny Oltepesi take the signposted left turn to **Olorgasailie Prehistoric Site**, 1½km (1 mile) away, where one of our earliest ancestors, *Homo erectus,* killed a group of giant baboon-like creatures using crude stone flints and left their remains and weapons to be discovered by Louis Leakey almost half a million years later. You can spend an hour or so visiting the site with a resident guide from the National Museum.

Drive on to the pink waters of **Lake Magadi**, 45km (28 miles) further south through the Ol Keju Ngiro Valley. The 100 sq-km (38 sq-mile) lake is only 580 metres (1,903ft) above sea level and is one of the world's richest sources of soda. Register your vehicle at the gate, then drive along the causeway and up to the T-junction. Turn right, then left and around the factory. Cross over another causeway and, after about 1km (½ mile), take the smaller of the two tracks leading straight ahead. After three more causeways, the track turns to the right, then sharply to the left. Leave your car at the bottom and walk up the track on the left to the viewpoint about ½km (¼ mile) away. It is a steep climb but the view is well worth it. Leave in good time to retrace your route back to Nairobi before dark (allow at least 3½ hours).

Alternatively, continue west from Magadi to the Nguruman Escarpment – a gruelling 64km (40 miles) of unmade road that demands a four-wheel-drive vehicle – for a two-night stay at either the luxurious **Shompole Lodge** (tel: 020-883280/883331; www.theartofventures.com) or the eco-friendly **Sampu Camp** (Let's Go Travel; tel: 020-4447151/4441030; www.lets-go-travel.net). They both sit on the edge of the escarpment, Shompole in a private conservancy and Sampu within Olkiramatian Group Ranch, and both have sploendid views over the Great Rift Valley.

14. THE MAASAI MARA *(see map, p44)*

A two-night trip to the Maasai Mara, including a balloon ride and a champagne breakfast, a luxury tented camp or lodge, beautiful scenery and the best wildlife in Kenya.

Before you leave Nairobi, you must book not only your accommodation and transport for game viewing but also your balloon flight. You must also pay all required entry fees for the Maasai Mara Reserve, Mara Triangle and/or conservancies surrounding the Mara before leaving the city. Ask your travel/tour agent about this when making your bookings. It is also possible to fly to the Mara from Wilson Airport; the flight takes 45 minutes.

Buy the Macmillan map of the Maasai Mara (in most Nairobi bookshops and hotels). It shows the major tracks and will give you some sense of direction in this 1,530 sq-km (590 sq-mile) reserve. The Mara's wide horizons are unforgettable and game are clearly visible. The best time to go is in July and August to see the Great Migration, when millions of wildebeest and other plains game migrate into the Mara. At any time of year

Above: braided hair and elaborate beaded necklaces are characteristic of the Maasai

you are more likely to see the Big Five – lion, buffalo, elephant, leopard and rhino – than in any other reserve.

Follow Itinerary 5, turning left at the end of the dual carriageway on to the B3, the old road to Naivasha, which winds down the Rift Valley escarpment and offers beautiful views over the valley floor and mountains Susua and Longonot. The tiny church nestling in the hillside near the bottom of the escarpment was built by Italian prisoners of war during World War II. A few kilometres after the church, turn left at Mai Mahiu village (but still on the B3) to Narok, 90km (56 miles) away. The road surface is good tarmac all the way.

Narok is the capital of Maasai country and is the last place where you can refuel before reaching the reserve. You can avoid the souvenir-sellers by driving through town and stopping at the first garage outside Narok on the right, at the top of the hill. You can also buy cold drinks, snacks and souvenirs here, or drop into the Seasons Hotel for refreshments. After Narok drive on for 20km (13 miles) to reach Ewaso Ngiro, where you cross the river of the same name.

In the rainy season (generally from the end of March to the beginning of June and mid-October to mid-November, but check current weather conditions) turn left at Ewaso Ngiro on to the tarmacked C12. This road becomes dirt after another 55km (34 miles) and leads to the east of the reserve, entering via the Sekenani Gate (about 4 hours from Nairobi).

Balloon Safari

Stay overnight at **Keekorok Lodge** (Wilderness Lodges; tel: 020-532329 or 050-22525/6; www.wildernesslodges.com), 23km (14 miles) from Sekenani Gate, which is always surrounded by plenty of wildlife. In the rainy season you can take your balloon safari from here. Alternatively, arrange to stay at **Siana Springs**, a lodge just outside the reserve that is run by Heritage Hotels (tel: 020-4446651/4442115 or 050-23023; www.heritage-eastafrica.com).

If conditions are dry, from Ewaso Ngiro go straight along the dirt road (C13), turn left on to the E176 (also a

Above: a hot-air balloon casts a shadow on the Mara
Right: an impala buck, with lyre-shaped horns

The Annual Migration

In April, about 1.6 million wildebeest gather on the Serengeti plains in Tanzania and prepare to journey north, following the rains, in search of new grazing and water. They are accompanied by zebra and gazelles. Early in July the enormous herds reach the Maasai Mara and spread out across the plains to forage for sustenance. Once the plains are grazed bare the animals move on, crossing the Mara River in the east of the reserve. Only the strongest survive the long treks. Weak animals either die of fatigue, drown in rivers or are hunted by predators. Towards mid-September the herds begin to gather in preparation for the crossing back into the Tanzanian plains where they arrive towards the end of December.

dirt road) and enter the reserve via the Ololoolo Gate to the west. This takes about 5½ hours from Nairobi. Stay at **Mara Safari Club** (tel: 020-216940; www.lonrhohotels.com) or at **Kichwa Tembo Tented Safari Camp** or **Bateleur Camp** (book these two through the Conservation Corporation, Nairobi; tel: 020-3745239/49; www. ccafrica.com). But it is no joke to be bogged down in the black cotton soil, and in wet conditions you may be stranded for some time, so try to avoid this area during the rainy season.

Dry-season travellers should book their balloon safari from **Governor's** or **Little Governor's Camp** (tel: 020-2734000; www.governorscamp.com). If you want to spend your time in the middle of the reserve, with great views over the migration corridor, stay at **Mara Intrepids** (bookings through Heritage Hotels, as above for Siana Springs).

It's impossible to be specific about where you'll see the various animals but, generally speaking, look for lion hunting close to bushes on the plains at dusk or sunrise; cheetah sitting on rocks on the open Burrungat plains; leopard in riverine forest; elephant near rivers and in swampy areas; and rhino in scrubby bush country (near the Burrungat plains). Buffalo are every-

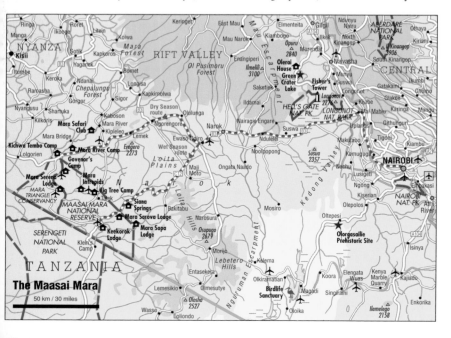

where, as are the various gazelles and antelopes, zebra, giraffe, warthog, topi etc. Bird life is abundant, with over 540 species to be found in this region.

There are several hippo pools along the Mara River, which flows through the reserve from north to south. Visit hippo at dusk when they stop wallowing in the mud and clamber out to graze. If you are staying outside the reserve, there is also the opportunity of evening game drives, giving you the chance to see nocturnal animals such as leopard, porcupine, spring hare, aardwolf, civet and genet.

Early next morning take a **balloon safari**. Take a hat to protect your head from the heat of the burner. Spend an hour drifting above the animals (marvellous photo and video opportunities) then land and enjoy a champagne breakfast out in the bush. This will undoubtedly be a highlight of your holiday and is well worth the expense (around US$395), if you can stretch to it. Afterwards you'll be driven back to your vehicle and can spend the rest of the day game-driving or resting at camp.

Keen anglers can try their hand at catching a giant Nile perch on a day's **fishing trip** to Lake Victoria: depart early in the morning from the Maasai Mara on a 40-minute flight and return in the afternoon in time for a game drive. Fishing trips are organised by Mfangano Island Camp (book through Governor's Camp, above) and Rusinga Island Lodge (book with Private Wilderness; tel: 020-882028/222598; www.privatewilderness.com).

15. MERU NATIONAL PARK AND LEWA WILDLIFE CONSERVANCY *(see map, p51)*

A four-night safari to an area that until recently was a forgotten part of Kenya and is still off the main tourist track. Includes a visit to Lewa Wildlife Conservancy, a pioneer in the conservation of wildlife and its habitat through income-generating projects supported and managed by local communities.

A four-wheel-drive vehicle is recommended, though the roads in the park are good when the weather is dry.

Meru National Park became world-famous with *Born Free*, the story of Elsa the lioness. It was here that Joy and George Adamson spent many years preparing orphaned cubs for rehabilitation into the wild. The park covers an area of 800 sq km (320 sq miles), to the west of Mount Kenya in the semi-arid area of the country. It straddles the equator and ranges in altitude from 1,000m (3,300ft) in the foothills of the Nyambeni Range (the western boundary) to less than 300m (990ft) on the Tana River in the south.

Right: a lioness and her cub in the golden light of early evening

To get to Meru, follow Itinerary 7 as far as Thika. Continue on the A2, then take the turn-off for Embu and Meru (B6), 86 km (53 miles) from Nairobi. Drive through Embu and continue on to Meru town. There are many potholes and numerous speed bumps on this very hilly stretch of road. Be sure to fill your car up in Meru and carry an extra 20 litres of petrol. Turn right at the BP petrol station in Meru onto the road to Maua (66 km/41 miles), north through the Nyambeni Hills. There are some spectacular views over the plains and rocky outcrops of Samburu, including the square-topped rocky massif of Ololokwe. There are many potholes along this road and you must also watch out for the Miraa transporters which rattle along at high speeds. The turn to the park is 5 km (3 miles) before Maua, off to the left 25 km (16 miles) down a bumpy murram road.

As you enter the park, follow the main road for the junction and follow the signpost to **Leopard Rock Lodge** (tel: 020-600031; www.leopardmico. com), attractively situated on a river that is home to crocodile and hippo. The lodge has spacious rooms with ensuite facilities and a swimming pool.

Alternatively, turn right to Park Headquarters and Mughwango Hill where the exclusive eight-cottage **Elsa's Kopje** (book through Cheli & Peacock, tel: 02-603090-1/604053-4; www.chelipeacock.com). Each of the stone and thatch cottages is individually designed to incorporate the rock's natural features, with breathtaking views over the plains of Meru. From here you can enjoy activities such as guided nature walks, fishing, night games drives and rafting on the Tana River. Self-catering accommodation is available at the Kenya Wildlife Service's **Bwatherongi and Murera Bandas** (KWS Marketing & Development; tel: 020-600800; www.kws.org).

There are all-weather airstrips at Meru Kinna, just outside the park, and at Meru Mulika Lodge (now closed down) about 4 km (2½ miles) from the Murera Gate inside the park. If you choose to fly to Meru, the charter company will choose which airstrip they will take you to: you will need to send your vehicle ahead to pick you up, or arrange to be collected by the staff of the lodge where you will be staying.

There are scheduled daily flights to Meru from Nairobi, Samburu, Lewa Downs, Nanyuki and the Maasai Mara on either AirKenya, SafariLink or Tropic Air. *See Practical Information, page 87.*

There is plenty of water in Meru – not just the Tana river, but many other small streams, swamps and underground springs coming off Mount Kenya. There are no large numbers of animals, due to heavy poaching in the past, but you will see rare species such as Grevy's zebra and reticulated giraffe. Usually you will find elephant and buffalo in or around swamps or smaller

Left: a Maasai giraffe, a species found only to the south of the Tana River

rivers. When you spot them, drive quietly and keep your engine running while you watch, as many of the animals are still unused to human visitors and very skittish. There are over 350 bird species, including the uncommon palm-nut vulture, the palm swift and, near the Tana River, Pel's fishing owl and the rare Peter's finfoot.

On your second day, ask your lodge to supply a picnic and plenty to drink, and drive down to **Adamson's Falls** on the Tana River, at least an hour's drive. (Take a Kenya Wildlife Service ranger with you to help find the way: you can arrange this through your lodge.) Take time to appreciate the beauty of the falls with the blocks of granite that have been weathered and watered into weird shapes. You can also do some fishing above or below the falls.

Conservation in Action

On the last morning in the park, have an early breakfast and order a packed lunch and drinks for your trip to Lewa Conservancy. Return to Meru town and turn right onto the B6 to Isiolo. Continue on past the junction to Nanyuki and a few kilometres further on look out for the entrance to **Lewa Wildlife Conservancy** (www.lewa.org). Follow instructions as per your booking to where you will stay. The choice is between Lewa Safari Camp (tel: 020-600457/609745; www.bush-and-beyond.com), Lewa House (tel: 064-31405; email: c.moller@lewa.org) and Wilderness Trails, the delightful Craig family home (tel: 020-600457/605108; www.bush-homes.co.ke).

Enjoy a game drive after tea, finishing with an evening sundowner overlooking the vast conservancy. Arrange an early morning game drive for the following day or, better still, book a ride. Riding on horseback among the game – it's best done before breakfast – is a wonderful way to get close to wildlife, particularly giraffes, as they don't seem to recognise your smell or shape when you're on horseback.

After breakfast, you can visit some conservation-orientated activities including Lewa-supported schools and community development programmes, and learn about the conservancy's rhino, Grevy's zebra and lion projects. After lunch, leave Lewa Wildlife Conservancy (by 2.30pm at the latest), turn right on to the main road, drive the few kilometres to the Nanyuki/Meru/Isiolo junction and turn right. Continue on to Nanyuki, stop for refreshments at Nanyuki Airfield and visit the Laikipia Tourism Information Centre (www.laikipia.org), then continue on to Nairobi.

Above: a Samburu *moran* or warrior with traditional adornment

16. LAIKIPIA ADVENTURE SAFARI *(see map, p51)*

A five-night adventure safari, starting with a choice of outdoor pursuits, a night in a log cabin on the northern slopes of Mt Kenya followed by a safari to the bush country of the Northern Frontier District.

This safari requires a four-wheel-drive vehicle. Book your accommodation with Let's Go Travel (tel: 020-4447151; www.letsgosafari.com) or Rift Valley Adventures (tel: 062-41027; www.riftvalleyadventures.com). When booking, choose between full-board (food included) and self-catering (you provide the food and drink at each lodge, although staff will cook your meals for you). To avoid all the driving, daily schedule flights from Nairobi are available with road transfers from the airstrips to your destination.

This safari travels through a large part of the Laikipia ecosystem, in which the Laikipia Wildlife Forum has pioneered conservation and wildlife-management programmes, including the development of community-owned tourism projects. Your first accommodation is one of these – **Ol Gaboli Community Lodge**, on the banks of the Ewaso Ngiro river (see www.laikipia. org/safari_riftvalleyadventures.htm).

Leave Nairobi following directions to Nanyuki as given in Itinerary 7. Turn left off the main road between the Caltex and Total service stations and drive out of town until you meet the road to Rumuruti. After 9km (6 miles) turn right on to the new tarmac road to Dol Dol. After 13km (8 miles) the tarmac gives way to dirt, but stay on this road across the Ewaso Ngiro river, and follow signs to Ol Gaboli Lodge (another 20km/12 miles). If you stay two nights, you can devote your day to the outdoor activities that are available – rock-climbing, abseiling, rafting, canoeing, wilderness trekking, mountain biking, cultural tours, nature walks and bush skills.

On the second morning, drive back through Nanyuki (buy provisions there) and continue on the A2 beyond Timau. Turn right just past the petrol station after Timau and drive on the dirt road up to the Kizita Gorge. After about 9km (6 miles), bear right at the Mt Kenya School of Adventure. After another 8km (5 miles), turn left on to a grassy track, which takes you the last 18km (11 miles) to Rutundu. This should take about 2 hours in dry weather. Leave your vehicle at the gorge and take a challenging 15-minute walk through the gorge to **Rutundu Log Cabins** that overlook Lake Rutundu. The cabins are surrounded by alpine moorland, giant groundsel and lobelia vegetation that attract a unique bird life. This is a nature lover's paradise with great fishing and hiking – a 2-hour walk further up the mountain to Lake Alice will provide opportunities for trout fishing. Fishing equipment is available.

The following morning leave after breakfast, drive back to the Nanyuki-Isiolo road, and turn right towards Isiolo. After the long steep descent off the mountain, at the T-junction turn left and continue to the signs for Lewa Conservancy on the left-hand side of the road (only a few kilometres). Drive through Lewa Conservancy and follow directions given with your booking to either **Il Ngwesi** or **Tassia Lodge**. Both lodges are rustically built using local materials with

Left: cheetah, the fastest predator of the plains
Right: desolate Lake Turkana, the 'Jade Sea'

conservation and preservation in mind and built by their respective communities. The views are spectacular looking towards Samburu, Shaba and Lolokwe Mountain. Game drives and guided bush walks are recommended, with either a bush breakfast or dinner included. You can visit the **Il Ngwesi Maasai Cultural Manyatta** to give you an insight into the history and traditions of the Maasai.

On the last morning, leave after breakfast retracing your route back through Lewa Conservancy, on to Nanyuki and Nairobi. Visit the Laikipia Tourism Information Centre in Nanyuki and stop for lunch at Barney's Café at the airfield, or drive on another 3 km (2 miles) to the Trout Tree Restaurant, built in a beautiful big Mugumo tree overlooking the trout hatchery.

17. A GRAND TOUR TO LAKE TURKANA *(see map, p51)*

An action-packed seven-day trip to Lake Turkana, incorporating many of the highlights covered in the other itineraries. It includes Samburu National Reserve, Maralal, Loyangalani, Baringo, Bogoria and Nakuru.

A less dramatic way to get to Lake Turkana is to charter a plane from Nairobi's Wilson Airport. The journey takes about 2 hours. See Practical Information on page 87 for charter companies.

This is the most exhilarating trip in Kenya but it requires a lot of planning. Attempt it only in a fully equipped, four-wheel-drive vehicle with spare tyres, jerry-cans of fuel, spare hoses and fan belts and water and emergency food supplies. It is advisable to tell the car-hire company if you are undertaking this trip, as they will help you to prepare for it. If possible, you should go in convoy with another vehicle and have an armed guard travelling with you due to the insecurity in the region. If you break down en route it may be some time before anyone passes by to help you. Be prepared for at least two long, hot days of rough driving. However, it's worth every bump to see the sunset over the Jade Sea.

Follow Itinerary 9 to **Samburu** (stay the first night) and then continue to **Maralal** (for the second night) about 180 km (112 miles) or a day's drive

Above: desolate Lake Turkana, the 'Jade Sea'

away, along fairly rough and corrugated roads through beautiful and seldom-visited countryside. Leave Samburu on the Marsabit road (A2) and turn left on to the C79 towards Wamba. Before Wamba, turn left on to the C78 to Lodungokwe.

From here, follow the signs to Kisima, 57km (36 miles) from Lodungokwe, and Maralal, 19 km (11 miles) further. Maralal, in the foothills of the Samburu Highlands, is the area's administrative headquarters. Many of the *Mau Mau* resistance leaders, including Kenyatta, were imprisoned here during the years leading up to independence *(see History, page 13)*. The streets are very dusty and the nights are so cold that roaring log fires are not only welcoming but a necessity.

Fill up with fuel and check your oil, tyres and water in Maralal the evening before setting off for Turkana. To reach **Maralal Safari Lodge** (tel: 020-211124/246826 or 065-62060/62417; www.angelfire.com/jazz/maralal), turn left at the first roundabout (on the corner with the police station), drive straight across the second roundabout, and the lodge is signposted from here. Recharge your camera or camcorder battery and order a picnic lunch at the lodge, and ask for an early-morning call so that you can leave by first light.

The dirt C77 road from Kisima continues north to Turkana via Poror, Moridjo, Marti, Baragoi, South Horr and finally Loyangalani on the lake shore. It's only 214km (133 miles) but the road drops over 1,000m (3,280ft) and deteriorates from corrugated and potholed dirt to a boulder-strewn track until the last 50km (31 miles) are little more than a broken trail over chunks of black lava. Take a break at **Baragoi**, about 97km (60 miles) away. Buy a soda and barter over the price of engraved gourds at one of the *dukas* (grocers).

Before South Horr, there is a road to the left that leads to **Tuum**, a seldom-visited village on the western slopes of Mount Nyiru. There is a popular 2- to 3-hour mountain climb up Mount Nyiru from Tuum with spectacular views of Lake Turkana, Suguta Valley and Lake Logipi.

Above: pelican, Lake Baringo

From Baragoi to **South Horr** is 41km (25 miles), then it's another 76km (47 miles) to **Loyangalani**, on the shore of Lake Turkana. The final leg to Loyangalani is the roughest of all. En route you'll pass Turkana, Samburu and Rendille people with their distinctive dress.

The Jade Sea

In Loyangalani, stay two nights at **Oasis Lodge** (tel: 020-600470 or sat phone: +8821651155395; www.oasis-lodge.com). By the time you arrive, all you'll want to do is jump in the pool and relax. If the weather is good, ask about visiting **South Island National Park**, 13km (8 miles) across the lake. This is not always possible as the wind that blows off Mount Kulal whips up storms that can capsize small craft. There's little on the island but volcanic ash and a few feral goats – in fact, this is probably the most barren place you will ever visit, although crocodiles lay eggs there.

The next day, explore Loyangalani town's few *dukas*. Ask one of the shop-keepers to fix up a guide who can take you later in the day to visit the El-Molo, the smallest tribe in Kenya who live a few kilometres north. Then walk out to the lakeside the huts of the Rendille people. It's possible to swim in the bitter, alkaline waters – but be careful, as there are crocodiles about.

In the afternoon, collect your guide (arrange his fee in advance – approximately 200 shillings is usually acceptable) and visit the El-Molo people. For a few shillings, pens or packets of biscuits you can take their photographs but it's polite to ask their permission first. Try to peep inside one of their domed grass huts and go down to the water's edge to see their makeshift craft.

Next day, drive back to Maralal, and on the sixth day head for **Baringo**, back the way you came along the C78 towards Samburu National Reserve. At Kisima, turn right on to the C77 signposted Rumuruti and Loruk. Shortly after Sukuta lol Marmar – 32km (20 miles) after Kisima – take

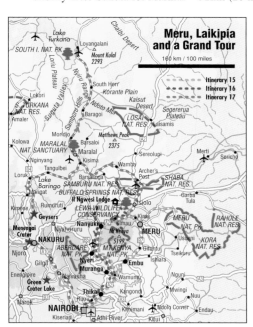

the right for Tangulbei, 45km (28 miles) further on. Drive through the village and take the left fork to Loruk about 5km (3 miles) later. This is a spectacular road across the Lerochi Plateau and down the northern end of Lake Baringo, where it joins the B4 to Nakuru.

Stay the night at Lake Baringo, at **Lake Baringo Island Camp** on Ol Kokwe Island *(see Itinerary 10 for details)*, then return to Nairobi the following morning via both Lake Bogoria and Lake Nakuru.

18. A SCENIC SAFARI THROUGH WESTERN KENYA
(see pull-out map)

A nine-day trip travelling north via the Rift Valley Lakes, then west through the dramatic Kerio Valley to Eldoret. On to Mt Elgon on Kenya's western border, southward to Kakamega Rain Forest then to Kisumu on Lake Victoria. Return to Nairobi with a visit to tea country at Kericho or via the Maasai Mara.

You will be driving mainly on tarmac roads, but some of these are quite rough. Roads in the parks are dirt, so a four-wheel-drive vehicle is recommended.

Follow Itinerary 10 to Lake Bogoria and stay at **Lake Bogoria Hotel** (tel: 051-2216441 or 020-249055; www.bogoriasparesort.com). The following morning, after an early morning game drive, ask for a packed lunch and leave soon after breakfast. Leave the reserve, drive 21 km (13 miles) along the E461 dirt road to the tarmacked B4 road from Nakuru to Loruk. Turn right and continue on to Marigat. Turn left here on to the C51 to Kabarnet – this is a winding escarpment up the side of the Rift Valley with amazing views. Carry on through Kabarnet and down into the Kerio Valley, stopping at **Sego Club** for lunch or refreshments. Continue on over the Chebloch Bridge and up the other side to Tambach and Iten. From Iten continue on to Eldoret. Stay overnight at the **Sirikwa Hotel** (tel: 053-2062499/2032117).

Start out early the next morning, stocking up on refreshments before leaving Eldoret. Head toward Kitale on the A104 to Malaba, then turn right onto the B2 to Kitale. On the A1 Kapenguria road, 23 km (14 miles) north of Kitale is **Barnley's House** (Let's Go Travel; tel: 020-4447154/4441030; www.letsgosafari.com). From here you can visit Kenya's smallest park, the **Saiwa Swamp National Park** (22 km/13 miles east of Kitale), home to the endangered semi-aquatic sitatunga antelope. Tree ladders and boardwalks offer good vantage points to view the animals and birds that live in the swamp and surrounding indigenous forest. Or stay at **Lokitela Farm**, 19 km (12 miles) west of Kitale in the foothills of Mt Elgon (contact Let's Go Travel, as above). Here you can explore a working farm which is also a birder's par-

adise. Visit **Mount Elgon National Park** and hike to the summit of the mountain or visit the **Kitum Caves** where elephants dig for salt. A two-night stay is essential to enjoy all that is on offer.

Leave Kitale after breakfast (not forgetting refreshments for the journey) to **Kakamega Forest National Reserve**. Follow the A1 to Webuye, where you turn left onto the A104 then after a short distance right on to the A1 to Malava and **Kakamega**. In Kakamega, turn left on to the road to Shinyalu, where you turn left again for the road to Kakamega Forest Reserve. Stay two nights at **Rondo Retreat Centre** (tel: 056-30268; www.rondoretreat.com) or **Isecheno Bandas** (Let's Go Travel, as above). The latter are very basic: you have to bring bedding and food. The forest is Kenya's only remnant of a massive forest that spread all over central and west Africa. It is an important bird area with over 330 species, including the magnificent great blue turaco, 440 butterfly species and many forest mammals. Make sure you see Mama Mutere, the tallest tree in the forest. There are rains storms most afternoons or early evening.

Fishermen and Tea Pickers

The following day, return to Kakamega and rejoin the A1 to **Kisumu**, Kenya's west coast city on Lake Victoria. Stay at the **Imperial Hotel** (tel: 057-2022211/7; www.imperialkisumu.com) or **Sunset Hotel** (tel: 057-2020464; email: hotelsunset1977@yahoo.co.uk). If you have time, visit **Ndere Island National Park**. Take the C27 towards Bondo, and after 25 km (16 miles), immediately after Holo Market, a dirt road leads to Bao Beach 50 km (31 miles) further on, where the Park HQ is located. Hire a boat from one of the local fishermen or, by prior booking, the KWS boat will take you to Ndere Island National Park. This is home to hippo, crocodile and a wide variety of birdlife, and you might have a rare sighting of a sitatunga. Back in Kisumu, visit the **Kisumu Impala Sanctuary** (near Hippo Point) which protects the last remaining stretch of lakeside forest in an area of less than 1 sq km (250 acres). It is home to a small herd of impala and has an animal orphanage.

Next morning leave Kisumu on the B1 and head for **Kericho**. Stay at **Weaver Cottage** (Let's Go Travel, as above), 6 km (4 miles) from town, situated in the lush green tea fields with views of the picturesque Nandi Hills. Or have lunch at the **Tea Hotel** and travel onto Nairobi via Nakuru.

Alternatively, drive from Kericho on the C23 to Sotik, turn left onto the B3 to Bomet and continue on to the Maasai Mara, to stay overnight at **Mara Safari Club** (tel: 020-216940 or 050-22170/2/3; www.lonrhohotels.com), entering via a private toll road from Mulot. See Itinerary 14 for other places to stay in the Mara. Leave the following morning taking the B3 to Narok and onto Mai Mahiu where you turn right on to the Naivasha–Nairobi road.

Left: entrance to Kitum Cave
Above: worker on a tea plantation

Mombasa
& the Coast

Haraka haraka haina baraka – an old Swahili proverb meaning 'Hurry hurry brings no blessing' – sums up the pace of life on Kenya's coast. The coastline stretches from Vanga, on the Tanzanian border in the south, to Malindi and Lamu in the north. Most of it is enclosed by a coral reef comprising four protected marine parks and home to more than 200 species of tropical fish. The reef is broken in only a few places, so shark, marlin and other big game fish rarely swim close to the beach. The water is always warm – around 27–35°C (80–95°F) – while the shade temperature is about 35°C (95°F) and tempered by the cooling monsoon breezes that blow year-round. If a tropical beach paradise is what you're after, Kenya's coast is hard to beat.

Arab Influences

Most of the itineraries in this section are based on Mombasa, a city whose eclectic history has left its mark in the old colonial Mombasa Club, tucked away in the Arab old town among narrow streets overhung with *mashrabia* (enclosed balconies), and Fort Jesus, built by the Portuguese but now a favourite film-set of Hollywood directors (witness *Beau Geste*) and a popular spot for tying the knot – around 80 couples a year marry here. Mombasa is Kenya's second largest city and serves as a port for several east and central African countries. Originally centred on the 14 sq-km (5½ sq-mile) island, the city has now spilled on to the mainland, which has developed as a centre for package tourism.

Mombasa's old town is interesting to visit for its Islamic architecture and people, but don't plan to spend more than one day here. For all its history, there's little to do apart from shop or pray, and the points of interest can be covered in half a day. To get the most out of the city, hire the services of a local guide (contact Southern Cross Safaris, tel: 041-474950; www.southerncrosssafaris.com). You will be taken to both the old and new town, and be shown the Indian temple, Fort Jesus and the shopping areas.

After that, jump in your car and leave the city behind. Our suggested itineraries include cruising on a dhow, visits to a crocodile farm, a nature park and a handicraft centre, game drives in Shimba Hills National Reserve and Tsavo East National Park, a trip to a coral reef to snorkel in the Indian Ocean, and a flight to Kenya's most picturesque town. All these journeys out of Mombasa start from the Elephant Tusks on Moi Avenue, close to the Castle Royal Hotel *(see map on page 56)*. If you would prefer a more restful base than Mombasa, take off to Watamu or Malindi *(see Itineraries 24 and 25)*, which can be reached by plane direct from Nairobi or Mombasa, or by car from Mombasa.

Left: the dhow was brought to East Africa by Arab traders
Right: see Maasai giraffe in the huge Tsavo East National Park

19. HILLS, FORESTS AND WATERFALLS *(see map, p58)*

Overnight excursion to Shimba Hills National Reserve, to see leopard baiting, elephants, rare sable antelope and Sheldrick Waterfalls.

This trip makes a cool change from the humidity of the coastal strip. Before setting out you should reserve accommodation at **Shimba Forest Lodge** (tel: 041-229608/0722-200952; www.aberdaresafarihotels.com) or **Travellers Mwaluganje Elephant Camp** (tel: 041-4585121/6; www.travellersbeach.com) . You'll need a four-wheel-drive vehicle.

Set off in the morning on the A14, cross Kilindini Harbour on the Likoni car ferry and drive south through the village of Waa. Shortly afterwards turn right on to the C106 leading to Kwale. The entrance to the **Shimba Hills National Reserve** is 3km (2 miles) after Kwale, along a good dirt road, and is well signposted. If you are staying at Shimba Forest Lodge, the resident 'hunter' will meet you at the park gates and accompany you on a game drive through the hilly coastal rainforest (rising up to 450m/1,475ft) and back to the lodge. The luxury Travellers Mwaluganje Elephant Camp is located in the elephant sanctuary in the National Reserve. From Kwale town, continue on the main dirt road (passing the main park entrance) for 15 km (9 miles), then turn right at the sign for the camp.

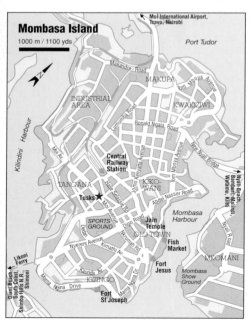

Mombasa Island
1000 m / 1100 yds

Above: Shimba Hills National Reserve has a resident herd of elephants

Shimba Hills National Reserve is one of the few game parks with an area set aside for walking, so make the most of the opportunity. Look out for the rare sable antelope with its distinctive long, curved horns – this is the only place in Kenya you will see them. You may also see buffalo, elephant, hyena, waterbuck, reedbuck, giraffe, baboon and perhaps lion.

You can take a strenuous 4-km (2½-mile) walk down to **Sheldrick Waterfalls**. Drive to the **Elephant Lookout**, walk down to the bottom of the valley, then follow the footpath through the trees, over the bridge and down to the falls. Be sure to make plenty of noise along the way to scare off any animals that might be thinking of drinking at the pool at the foot of the falls.

If you are staying at the lodge, follow your late-afternoon game drive with cocktails in the treehouse bar above the baited water-hole (all the bedrooms also face this), where you'll see lots of water birds, probably elephant and perhaps a leopard. The water-hole is floodlit at night – the animals have become accustomed to the idea of being permanently on stage. There's also a beautiful view down to Diani Beach.

Next morning take an early drive to see the sun rise over the Indian Ocean. Return to your lodge or camp for breakfast before heading back to Mombasa.

20. CROCODILES AND CRAFTS *(see map , p56)*

An afternoon excursion from Mombasa to Mamba Crocodile Village, Haller Park and Bombolulu Handicrafts Centre, followed by a night cruise and dinner on the *Tamarind* dhow.

Reserve your table on the Tamarind dhow a few days in advance (tel: 041-474600-2; www.tamarind.co.ke). Ask to be collected and returned to your hotel so that you don't have to drive at night.

Drive out of town along Moi Avenue towards Mombasa Harbour and turn left on to Digo Road which soon becomes Abdel Nasser Road. Turn left on to Tom Mboya Avenue, then right on to the B8 to cross the harbour on the New Nyali Bridge. Your first destination is the **Mamba Crocodile Village** (open daily 8am–6pm; tel: 041-475180), close to Nyali Beach opposite Nyali Golf Club. Turn right off the B8 on to the E982 and follow the signs. Plan to spend at least an hour here – there are hundreds of crocodiles of all sizes, as well as horse-riding, botanical gardens and a restaurant serving crocodile meat.

From Mamba, take the E982 north up the coast to the junction with the main road (B8) from the New Nyali Bridge. Continue north, towards Malindi, and shortly after the junction, on the left you'll see the entrance to **Haller Park** (open 2–5.30pm; tel: 041-5485901-4; www.lafargeecosystems.com). This is an excellent example of land reclamation. What was once Africa's largest cement quarry has been transformed into a timber plantation and nature park, complete with buffalo, warthog, eland, oryx, monkeys

Right: the brooding bulk of Fort Jesus, built in Mombasa by the Portuguese in 1593

and numerous birds as well as a fish farm, reptile pit, butterfly pavilion and plant nursery with indigenous tree species. An essential sight is Owen, the young hippo that was washed down the coast at Malindi following the Asian tsunami, and his close friend, Mzee, the 130-year-old Aldabran tortoise.

On leaving Bamburi, drive back towards Mombasa, stopping off at the **Bombolulu Handicrafts Workshop** (open Mon–Sat 8am–6pm; tel: 041-471704/473571; www.apdkbombolulu.com) off the B8: follow the bright yellow signs. This workshop was set up to employ handicapped Kenyans (who would otherwise be begging on the streets of Mombasa) making jewellery, wood carvings and leather-work. It is a good place to watch skilled artisans at work and you know your money will be going directly to the craftsmen and women. Allow enough time to return to your hotel, change for dinner (casual but smart) and pick up your transport to take you to the *Tamarind*.

Dhow Sailing

The dhow leaves at 6.30pm on the dot. You can watch the sun set as you sip your cocktail and cruise past old Mombasa town and Fort Jesus and into Tudor Creek. The dhow will moor here while you eat – and you'd better be hungry. It serves the best seafood, including lobster and crab, you're likely to get anywhere on the coast, though there's steak too for non-fish eaters. Afterwards you can dance to the music of the on-board band or just sit back and savour the night air. It's all a bit touristy, but no less enjoyable for that. The dhow returns to the jetty at 10.30pm.

An alternative evening's diversion is the **Dhow Sundowner Cruise** (Severin Sea Lodge, tel: 041-5487365; www.severin-kenya.com). The cruise, along the shores of Mombasa Island, concludes at the 16th-century Fort Jesus, where a sound and light show re-creating the turbulent history of the East African coast is followed by a candelabra-lit dinner within the fort.

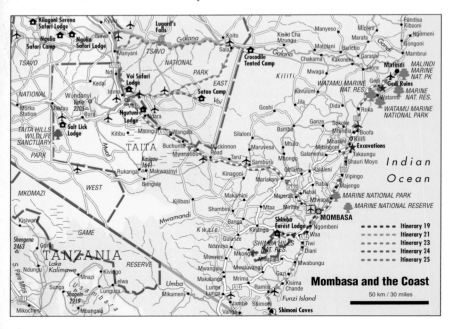

Mombasa and the Coast

50 km / 30 miles

Itinerary 19
Itinerary 21
Itinerary 23
Itinerary 24
Itinerary 25

21. KISITE-MPUNGUTI CORAL REEF *(see map, p58)*

A full-day excursion from Mombasa, with a road trip to Shimoni and a cruise in a motorised dhow to Kisite-Mpunguti Marine Reserve, which offers the best snorkelling in Kenya. Enjoy a five-course seafood lunch on Wasini Island followed by a visit to community projects and coral gardens. Take a sun hat, canvas shoes and bread (to feed the fish).

For reservations, contact Charlie Claw's Kisite Marine Park Dhow Tours; tel: 040-3202331/3203055/0722-205154; www.wasini-island.com.

If you don't want to drive, ask to be collected from your hotel when you make your reservation. If you drive, take the A14 out of Mombasa towards the Tanzanian border. Cross on to the mainland via the Likoni car ferry, then head south – there's only one road so you can't get lost. On the way you pass through villages belonging to the Digo tribe, including Waa, Tiwi, Diani, Ukunda, Msambweni and Ramisi, as well as cashew, coconut and sugar plantations. About 3km (2 miles) past Ramisi turn left on to the D543 to **Shimoni**. In Kiswahili, Shimoni means 'Place of the Hole' and is named after the 15-km (9-mile) long cave where slaves were imprisoned before being shipped out. Shimoni is 75km (46 miles) from Mombasa.

The dhow leaves Shimoni jetty at 9am. You can hire snorkelling equipment here. To make sure your snorkel mask fits properly, hold it against your face without the strap, breathe in and look down at your feet. If the mask stays in place it will not leak; if it falls off you need to try another one.

Snorkelling and Seafood

It's a 30-minute cruise to get to **Kisite-Mpunguti Marine Reserve**. Look out for dolphins on the way. The limpid waters here are the clearest along the coast, which makes for ideal snorkelling conditions. Spend the morning swimming among the numerous species of coral fish – they'll swim closer if you bring bread to feed to them – or relaxing on the dhow. Sightings of dolphins and turtles are almost guaranteed. Use plenty of sunblock and wear a T-shirt to protect yourself from the sun.

The exercise will whet your appetite for the five-course seafood lunch on **Wasini Island**. Just 5km (3 miles) long and 1km (½ mile) wide, Wasini used to be used as a shooting range in World War I and you can still find bits of scrap metal along the shore. Remember it's illegal to take shells off the beach. After lunch, visit the **Shimoni Slave Caves** community project and the **Wasini Women's Boardwalk** through the **coral gardens**, and watch traditional weavers at work in their shop (women should cover up to avoid offending the locals).

Above: a coconut plantation on the way to Shimoni
Right: marine life can be admired – but not removed

22. LAMU ISLAND *(see pull-out map)*

A day trip by plane to Lamu Island, visiting a museum and a donkey sanctuary and taking a dhow trip through mangrove swamps. Take a barbecued seafood lunch and explore an ancient Arab town.

The best time to be in Lamu is during the week-long Maulidi (Prophet's birthday) celebrations (variable date between April and June). Muslims from all over East Africa flock to take part in the religious festivals, dancing, sword fights and feasts. Be sure to reserve your accommodation in advance.

You'll either love or hate Lamu, the oldest town in Kenya, but you should definitely pay it a visit. Once a powerful, independent Swahili city state, this island situated 222km (138 miles) north of Malindi used to be so far off the beaten track that life there remained unchanged for centuries. Then in the 1970s the hippies arrived and Lamu has never looked back. Today the two cultures survive in uneasy symbiosis, paradoxically supported by the tourism that threatens both lifestyles.

But despite the *bangi* (marijuana) chewing dudes who pester every foreigner who walks the harbour front, Lamu still exudes a tranquil charm.

The only car on the island belongs to the District Officer – everyone else uses donkeys, dhows and their own two feet to get about. The most obvious aspect of the Muslim culture (apart from the numerous mosques) is the absence of alcohol – only one or two hotels sell it. And the most common form of dress is a long white *kanzu* (gown) for men and the black *bui-bui* (ankle-length cloak) for women.

Swahili Culture

To get to Lamu, take the morning flight from Malindi or Mombasa to **Manda Island**. There are several airlines and they all operate similar schedules *(see Practical Information, page 87)*. From Manda take the ferry across to **Lamu town**. Walk along the jetty, turn right and stroll along the harbour front for about 250m (270 yds), past the Tourist Information Bureau and Standard Chartered Bank until you reach the **Lamu Museum** (open daily 8am–6pm). This is an excellent introduction to Swahili culture, and is one of the best museums in Kenya. Exhibits on display include a reconstruction of a Swahili house, dhows and intricately carved ivory *siwa* (traditional ceremonial musical instruments).

Come out of the museum and continue to walk along the harbour front. A few blocks further on you'll come to the **Donkey Sanctuary** where decrepit, sick or old donkeys enjoy a comfortable retirement. Walk 200m (220 yds) beyond the donkeys and you can watch the wood-carvers at work making the intricately carved doors and lintels for which Lamu is famous.

Retrace your steps towards the jetty. On the way, haggle with the locals for a dhow to sail you to **Shela Beach** on the southernmost tip of the island, and back. The going rate is around Kshs 50 per person. Ask to see the man-

Above: a dhow sails through the mangrove swamps
Above right: traditional carved doors. **Right:** basket-weaving outside the mosque

grove swamps on the way (though whether you can or not depends on the wind speed and direction). Stop off at **Peponi Hotel** for an ice-cold beer and other drinks (Peponi's has a liquor licence) and have lunch in Peponi's Barbecue Grill (excellent seafood).

Spend an hour or so on the beach and potter round the town. Eighteenth-century Arab houses tower over narrow streets, hiding inner courtyards where fountains play behind intricately carved screens. Visit the market, where you will notice stalls selling betel nuts wrapped in leaves and wodges of *miraa* – both mild but addictive stimulants.

Tourist shops have replaced many of the traditional craft shops but you can still find carved wood, silver jewellery and cowhorn *siwas*. Spend your last hour poking around, but don't be late for your flight. Small planes have to land back at Malindi before sundown: if your departure is delayed you will be stranded on Lamu until next day.

If you want to prolong your visit, buy the map/leaflet *Lamu: Map & Guide to the Archipelago, the Island and the Town* at the museum bookshop and stay at Peponi (tel: 042-633421/0722-203082; www.peponi-lamu.com) or the Kijani House Hotel (tel: 042-633235/0733-545264; www.kijani-lamu.com), both on Shela Beach.

You'll find plenty of things to do. Take a dhow trip to **Pate Island** 32km (20 miles) to the northeast of Lamu (talk to the dhow captains along the harbour front), visit the **Swahili House Museum**, a traditional house that has been lovingly restored, or take a boat to **Matondoni** village to see dhow-makers and basket-weavers.

23. TSAVO EAST NATIONAL PARK *(see map, p58)*

Overnight trip to Tsavo East National Park, taking in elephants, crocodiles and plains game.

From Mombasa, drive along Moi Avenue and turn left into Digo Road. Turn left again into Jomo Kenyatta Avenue, straight on at the roundabout and continue over the Makupa causeway, towards Nairobi on the A109. Keep heading straight for 151km (94 miles) until you reach Voi. On the way, look out for baobab trees which look as if they have been planted upside down with their roots in the air. After the rains, you may see them in flower.

Turn right just before the petrol stations on the main road, and drive through Voi town following the signs towards the Voi Gate and **Voi Safari Lodge** (tel: 043-30019/30027; www.kenya-safari.co.ke), where you can stay. Take the road to the left after the park entrance and drive uphill for 10km (6 miles) to get to the lodge. Watch out for fringe-eared oryx on the way. Before lunch, take a swim in the pool and look for elephant at the watering-hole.

For more personalised accommodation, stay at **Satao Camp** (Southern Cross Safaris; tel: 043-30415 or 041-475074-6; www.sataocamp.com), 30 minutes east of Voi Safari Lodge and situated on the seasonal Voi River, overlooking a watering-hole. Get there through Bachuma Gate, via bollards 143, 149 and 144.

Largest in Africa

The Tsavo East and West National Parks comprise one of the largest game parks in the world, covering an area of 21,283 sq km (8,148 sq miles) or 4 percent of Kenya's landmass (you are in Tsavo East – Tsavo West is on the other side of the Nairobi–Mombasa road). There was mass poaching here in the 1970s and 1980s, which reduced the elephant population from around 55,000 to just 5,000 and the rhino population from 7,000 to fewer than 50. However, armed wardens and rangers trained by the British SAS (Special Air Service) and with a shoot-to-kill policy towards poachers have proved ef-

Above: Tsavo's black rhino population was reduced to 50 by poaching, but it is now increasing slowly

fective in curbing the slaughter, and now numbers are on the increase again. There are more than 1,000 plant species and over 60 large mammal species. This park has well-graded roads with numbered bollards at each junction so, despite its huge size, it is quite easy to navigate.

After lunch, take a game drive along the river or relax and bird-watch by the Voi Safari Lodge swimming-pool. After tea, climb to the top of the cliff behind the lodge for views of the endless plains to the east and northeast.

Next morning drive 24km (15 miles) north past Irima and Magengani waterholes to Mudanda Rock (via bollards 165, 147, 158, 166). It juts up above a dam where thousands of animals gather in the dry season. Drive back to bollard 158 and then head north for 50km (31 miles), past the Buffalo Wallows (bollard 169), to **Lugard's Falls** and **Crocodile Point** (bollards 160, 161, 162). Drive east to bollard 163, then turn south along Rhino Ridge to bollard 107 and bollard 138 for **Aruba Dam** and Lodge. The reservoir created by Aruba Dam measures 85 hectares (210 acres) and is popular with elephant and plains game.

Turn right to get back to Voi, via the Kandera Swamp, and then retrace your route from here to Mombasa. Remember to leave enough time to get back to Mombasa before nightfall. Alternatively, you can turn right at Voi to drive on to Nairobi, 333km (217 miles) away. To arrive in Nairobi before sunset allow at least 5 hours for the journey. It is a long and tiring drive.

24. WATAMU *(see map, p58)*

A morning drive to Watamu, where you will stay.

Though Watamu, along with Malindi (see Itinerary 25), can be visited from Mombasa, it makes a very agreeable base, particularly if you prefer a quieter scene than the one in Mombasa. This itinerary is therefore designed as a linear rather than circular tour, and assumes you will want to stay in Watamu for a few days. The drive takes about 2 hours.

From Mombasa, cross over Nyali Bridge to the mainland and drive north up the B8. It's a beautiful drive, passing by baobab trees, palms, a sisal estate and numerous mosques. **Kilifi Creek**, 59km (37 miles) to the north, is spanned by a bridge built by the Japanese and opened in 1992. You can stop in Kilifi town on the northern side of the bridge to buy salted nuts and sodas for the journey.

You're now 64km (40 miles) from Malindi. To get to Watamu, head north and turn right at the Gedi turn-off on to the E899. It is well signposted. This road will take you past the entrance to the Gedi Ruins *(see Itinerary 25)* and on to Watamu village.

Despite the influx of tourism, **Watamu** has lost little of its sleepy, fishing village atmosphere. You can still see fishermen paddling ashore in their makeshift dhows and you won't be bombarded by the ubiquitous beach touts trying to sell you things that you don't really want. There's not much to do in the village itself (except buy groceries and curios and post letters), although it is interesting to contrast the simplicity of the local

Right: the Sokoke scops owl is found in the Arabuku-Sokoke Forest Reserve near Watamu

people's lifestyle and tumbledown *makuti* (palm-thatched) cottages with the opulence of the five tourist hotels lining the beach to the south.

Hemingway Haunt

Undoubtedly, the best hotel on this stretch of the coast is **Hemingways** (tel: 042-32624/32276; www.hemingways.co.ke). The hotel is named after Ernest Hemingway, who used to pursue his obsession with deep-sea fishing from this bay. In fact, this part of the Indian Ocean is still the haunt of craggy old fishermen recounting endless tales of the one that got away. The hotel's Deep Sea Fishing and Watersports Centre can arrange horse-riding (8.30–10.30am, 4–5pm and 5.30–6.30pm), tennis, golf (at Malindi Golf and Country Club), camel treks, bird-watching, waterskiing and a barbecue on Mida Creek.

   Turtle Bay Beach Club (tel: 042-32003/32622; www.turtlebay.co.ke) or **Ocean Sports Hotel** (tel: 042-32008/32288; www.oceansports.net) will arrange a guided tour for you through the **Arabuko-Sokoke Forest Reserve**, a few kilometres inland from Watamu. The forest covers over 320 sq km (124 sq miles) and is home to various mammals, from elephants to elephant shrews, as well as birds (including the Sokoke scops owl and the Sokoke pipit) and hundreds of insects and butterflies.

   If you are keen on reptiles, visit the **Bio-Ken Snake Farm** (tel: 042-32265/32303; email: snakes@africaonline.co.ke). It has one of the largest collections of snakes in East Africa, and you can join a fascinating Snake Spotting Safari around the Watamu area.

Above: traditional boat in Watamu bay

25. MALINDI *(see map, p58)*

A full-day excursion to Malindi from Watamu, taking in Gedi Ruins, snakes and butterflies, and swimming or relaxing at a beach club.

Providing you don't mind pedalling against the wind in one direction, this is a great bicycle trip (hire cycles from Watamu village).

From Watamu, drive (or cycle) back for about 2½km (1¾ miles) along the E899 towards Gedi. Turn off along a gravel road on the right just before the T-junction. The **Gedi Ruins** are 1km (½ mile) further along.

The crumbled remains of this Arab-Swahili town are built out of coral and are believed to date back to the 13th century. They were discovered in the 1920s and the site is still surrounded by Tarzanesque jungle, with lizards, monkeys and butterflies darting among the crumbling stones. There are the remains of a palace, several mosques, tombs and houses with painted plaster walls. Most surprising of all are the remnants of seemingly modern bathrooms with double washbasins and bidets. Allow at least an hour to visit the site; you can buy an excellent guidebook and map at the entrance. Just next door is the **Kipepeo Butterfly Farm** (tel: 042-32380; www.kipepeo.org), a conservation and breeding centre that is open to the public.

Afterwards return to the E899 and turn right. At the T-junction, turn right again on to the B8 and drive towards Malindi town. Go past the airport and bear left at the roundabout. At the next T-junction (with the Police Station on the left and the Post Office on the right) turn right up the hill. At the next crossroads (with the District Commissioner's office on the left and small public garden on the right), turn left on to the coast road to reach the **Pillar Tombs**, on the right next to the Juma Mosque. The **Malindi Museum** (open daily 9.30am–6pm; admission fee), known as the House of Columns, is a bit further on past the fish market. Among its exhibits is a coelacanth, a prehistoric fish found near Malindi in 2001. Further along the road, stop at the little Portugese **Chapel of St Francis Xavier**. A couple of hundred metres after the chapel, on Vasco Da Gama Point, is the **Vasco Da Gama Cross**, one of the oldest European monuments in Africa (1498).

By now you'll be hot and in need of a swim and refreshments. Head for the **Driftwood Beach Club** – turn left on to the seafront road and continue past Coral Keys Hotel and Silversands Campsite. Just after the campsite, about 200m (220 yards) along a dirt road, is the Beach Club. The small temporary membership fee entitles you to swim in the pool (or ocean) or relax at the bar.

A Closer Look at Reptiles

There's one more attraction in Malindi, the **snake park**, best visited around 4pm (many of the residents are comatose in the heat of the day). Turn left out of the Driftwood and continue to the tarmac road. Turn left here and continue for a kilometre or so until a left turn to the marine park. The turning to the snake park is on the right: just follow the signs. On view are numerous reptiles, including a pancake tortoise, from Turkana.

To return to Watamu, retrace your path to the main road and continue to the roundabout with a Total petrol station on the left. Take the first left at the roundabout for the main B8 road to Gedi, Watamu or Mombasa.

Leisure *Activities*

SHOPPING

Baskets and Textiles

The ubiquitous woven sisal baskets known as *kiondos* are everywhere. They're very useful, and thief-proof for carrying valuables around. Also common are Kisii soapstone carvings, soap dishes and bowls (either in natural pink and white or, the latest fashion, brightly painted and engraved), and wood carvings depicting animals and Kenyan tribespeople; look out for the - Giacometti-like figures carved out of a single branch.

Brightly coloured textiles include batiks, on silk or cotton, and cotton *kangas* and *kikois*, traditionally worn as wrap-arounds for men and women, but also great for scarves, throws or cushion covers back home.

Hand-woven cloth and rugs in cotton or wool are coloured with natural or synthetic dyes. Buy tablecloths, napkins, bedspreads or simply reams of fabric to cover furniture, make cushions, etc.

Less traditional but very characteristic are T-shirts. Look for the colourful designs of One Way or Dash.

Jewellery and Glass

Traditional and modern designs incorporate silver, amber, shells, coral, copper wire, leather, feathers, etc. Semi-precious stones (red and green garnet, malachite, tiger eye etc) are also used. On the coast, you will find Arab designs in silver. For glassware, look out for hand-blown goblets and other tableware reminiscent of medieval drinking vessels in thick blue or green glass full of air bubbles made by Kitengela Glass: outlets at Limuru Road, The Junction Shopping Centre, Ngong Road, and Adams Arcade, Ngong Road.

Woodwork

Zanzibari chests, originally from Zanzibar but now available all along the East African coast, come in various sizes. They are intricately carved out of *mvuli* wood with brass or silver bindings, studs and locks. You will also find attractive desks and coffee tables in similar designs.

Equally handsome are carved beds originating in Lamu. These look wonderful with lots of *kikoi-* and *kanga*-covered cushions. To solve transportation problems, you can buy just the carved legs in Kenya then have the finished article assembled back home.

Hand-made wooden picture frames and trays are attractive, some inlaid with brass.

Where to Shop

Nairobi

Maasai markets

An open-air Maasai market is held every Friday from around 9am to 5pm at the Village Market on Limuru Road, Gigiri, where you can buy tribal artefacts such as spears, shields, gourds, masks, cowbells and items of jewellery.

Similar markets are held every Tuesday, 9am to 5pm, at the Globe Roundabout (north of Nairobi, where Moi Avenue intersects with Muranga Road) and every Sunday at Yaya Centre, Argwings Kodhek Road, Kilimani.

City Market

Between Muindi Mbingu and Koinange Streets
Open Monday to Friday 7.30am–6pm, Saturday 7.30am–4pm, Sunday 8am–1pm. For fruit, vegetables, crafts, baskets, Kisii soapstone carvings, batiks etc.

Left: Maasai shields for souvenirs
Right: weaving *kiondo* baskets

For a wide selection of ceramic beads, a trip to **Kazuri Beads** in Karen is worth the effort. They also have outlets at Village Market, Limuru Road, and The Junction Shopping Centre, Ngong Road. For safari wear, try **Colpro** on Kimathi Street and **Legend Lives Ltd** at Wilson airport. In addition, Nairobi has a wide range of art, curio and souvenir shops. Here are a few:

Gallery Watatu
Lonrho House, Standard Street
Open daily 9.30am–6pm.
A diverse collection of Kenyan art includes sculptures and paintings by internationally recognised artists, such as Jak Katarikawe and Sane Wadu, as well as talented newcomers. Talk to the knowledgeable sales assistants: they have a genuine love for African art. Prices start at around 1,500 shillings but can soar.

African Heritage
Libra House, Mombasa Road
Open Monday–Friday 9.30am–6pm, Saturday 9.30am–10pm, Sunday 11am–4pm.
Also at the Carnivore Restaurant, Langata Road
Open daily noon–11pm.
Both branches have extensive collections of arts and crafts from all over Africa, including furniture, masks, carvings, paintings and batiks, baskets, jewellery and religious icons.

These are not the cheapest places to shop but the quality is superb – come here before going to other craft markets. The Libra House shop, on the road to the airport, is mind-boggling: you'll probably spend more than you planned.

Sarang Art Gallery
Stanley Hotel, Standard Street
Open Monday–Saturday 9am–5.30pm. Similar to Gallery Watatu but not as expensive. Good collection of wood and stone sculptures.

Kazuri Beads
Mbagathi Ridge, Karen
Nairobi outlets: Village Market, Limuru Road; Viking House, Waiyaki Way, Westlands; The Junction Shopping Centre, Ngong Road. Coast outlets: Diani Shopping Centre and Bombolulu
Open Monday–Friday 8am–4.30pm, Saturday 8.30am–4.30pm, Sunday 11am–4.30pm.
For a wide selection of ceramic beads and Africana pottery ware.

Kashmir Crafts
Biashara Street (near Moktar Daddah Street)
Open Monday–Friday 8.30am–12.30pm and 2–5.30pm, Saturday 8.30am–12.30pm and 1.30–4.30pm.
If you can't find what you want, talk to

Above: all manner of artefacts in traditional style for sale in Mombasa

Ramesh – he can unearth just about anything and his prices are very competitive. Ask to see his carved Zanzibari chests, made by his cousin in Mombasa. He has a wonderful collection of jewellery and can make up earrings, necklaces, rings and brooches at very reasonable prices.

The Spinner's Web
Viking House, Waiyaki Way, Westlands
Open Monday–Saturday 9am–6pm.
Stocks a huge selection of professional-quality crafts including pottery, hand-woven rugs, wallhangings, clothes, jewellery, home furnishings and accessories, as well as hand-painted trays, carved salad servers, boxes, beaded bowls etc.

Undugu Shop
Woodvale Grove, Westlands
(around the corner from the market)
Open Monday–Friday 9am–5.30pm and Saturday 9am–5pm.
Undugu means 'brotherhood' in Kiswahili and this shop was founded to help unemployed youths. The arts and crafts sold here are locally made and are similar to those at the Spinner's Web. They are excellent quality and usually much cheaper than elsewhere. Profits go towards community homes for street children, preventive health care, training etc.

Blue Rhino
ABC Place, Waiyaki Way, and Village Market, Limuru Road
Open Monday–Saturday 9am–6pm and Sunday 9am–1pm.
Great selection of traditional and contemporary products including paper products, photograph albums, T-shirts, ornaments and illustrated maps.

Utumaduni
(Crafts for Conservation)
Bogani East Road off Langata Road
(near the Giraffe Sanctuary), Langata
Open every day 9.30am–6pm.
This enormous house has different boutiques in each room, including a children's toy shop and play area, an art and crafts outlet, a tea room and an art gallery. Good for lunch.

Right: wood-carvings often display superb craftsmanship

The Glass Gallery
Karen Blixen Coffee Garden, 336 Karen Road, Karen
Open Monday–Saturday 9am–6pm.
Possibly the most elegant shop in Nairobi. Resident artist Pippa Simpson engraves African images on glass goblets, vases, perfume bottles, mirrors, bowls etc. Discuss your design with her personally.

There is also a range of stained-glassware on offer, including window panels and lampshades, and lovely antique silver jewellery. All purchases can be shipped home for you on request.

Haria's Stamp Shop
Biashara Street
Open Monday–Friday 8.30am–5.30pm and Saturday 9am–5pm. Closed for lunch 1.30–2pm every day.
One of the best-known souvenir shops in Nairobi. Despite its name, you can buy *kangas, kikois,* cards, carvings, T-shirts, safari clothes and many souvenir items.

Legend House
Entrance to Wilson Airport
Open Monday–Saturday 8.30am–5.30pm.
Stocks safari clothes and artwork by local

artists. Items include carpets, paintings, mirrors, antiques and furniture.

The Banana Box
Sarit Centre, Westlands
Good-quality souvenirs, including jewellery, glass, baskets and picture frames.

Zebu
The Junction Shopping Centre,
Ngong Road
Maasai beaded items, including belts, bags, shoes and jewellery.

Artz
Village Market, Limuru Road
A varied collection of paintings and sculptures by well-known local artists. Prices are very reasonable.

Laikipia Outpost
Nanyuki Airfield, Nanyuki
An assorted range of gifts and souvenirs.

Mutumaiyu Gift Shop
Nanyuki Main Street, near Barclays Bank,
Nanyuki

On the Coast
In Mombasa, browse round the shops along Biashara Street. There are also lots of handicraft stalls, with wood and soapstone carvings, hats and other textiles, beads, bangles, and *kiondos* near the hotels. The shops near the Serena Beach Hotel on North Beach (turn right out of the hotel) have some wonderful old wooden statues, headdresses, stools and tables from all over Africa, but their prices are very inflated. Good places to go are **African Heritage,** which has a shop in the Serena Beach Hotel, and **Bombolulu Workshop and Cultural Centre** on Malindi Road.

In the main tourist centres along the coast, including hotels, there are many small shops offering a large variety of gifts, souvenirs, *kikois, kangas,* Maasai beaded items, carvings, baskets, clothes and shoes.

Tatun Arts
Coral Key Beach Resort, Malindi
Good quality gift items.

Gallery Baraka
Lamu Island
Assorted range of gifts and souvenirs.

Above: women selling *kangas* on a Mombasa beach

EATING OUT

Traditionally, Kenyans breakfast on *mandazi* (a triangular-shaped doughnut) washed down with sweet milky tea. Lunch is *ugali* (corn meal porridge) eaten with vegetable or meat stew. Dinner might be *nyama choma* (grilled meat, often goat) and *sukuma wiki* (spinach). Other dishes include *irio* (soaked green peas cooked with potatoes and maize) and *githeri* (red beans and maize with potatoes, carrots, spinach, tomatoes and onions). They're all worth trying but will not necessarily please palates used to more piquant flavours.

Though the national cuisine is somewhat bland, the wide and delicious range of other foods on offer more than makes up for it. Fish-eaters can indulge in lobster, prawns, crayfish, Nile perch, *tilapia* (a freshwater fish similar to perch), parrot fish or delicious smoked sailfish, the Kenyan equivalent to smoked salmon. Meat-eaters can eat their fill of zebra, gazelle, crocodile, giraffe, ostrich, or the rather more ordinary beef or Molo lamb. Healthy eating enthusiasts can tuck into passion fruit, paw-paw, guavas, pineapple, plums, oranges, bananas and other fruits. To see and sample the wide range of fresh produce on offer, you should call into Nairobi's City Market *(see Shopping)*.

No one should miss warm toasted cashew nuts, macadamia nuts and coconuts, or avocados with Worcestershire sauce. Or plantain, arrowroot or cassava chips. And so the list goes on.

On the drinking front, the leading Kenyan beers are Pilsner, Tusker, White Cap, Tusker Malt Lager and Tusker Keg. European brands such as Heineken and Guinness are also brewed here. Kenya Cane is a white rum made from sugar cane, similar to Bacardi. Kenya Gold is a coffee liqueur.

Attempts were made to grow wine-producing grapes near Naivasha, but were abandoned when South African and European wines began to flood the market. Imported wine in restaurants is expensive by Kenyan standards, but not excessively so for European or American visitors. Wine in supermarkets is reasonably priced, considering how far it has travelled.

Eating out is one of the great pleasures of Kenya. There are plenty of excellent restaurants in Nairobi and, at most of them, you'd be hard pressed to spend much more than 1,000 shillings (£7–8) per person excluding wine, although at a few of the really expensive places you could pay three times as much, with appetisers and dessert.

If you're looking for a quick snack, a number of Nairobi's shopping centres (Sarit, Yaya, ABC Place, Village Market) have a selection of restaurants or food courts offering local dishes, salad bars, Italian, European, Indian and fast foods.

Nairobi
Meat and Seafood
Mandhari Restaurant
Serena Hotel, Kenyatta Avenue
Tel: 020-2822000/2725111
Open daily 12.30–3.30pm and 7.30–11pm. Elegant and intimate restaurant with superb international cuisine. Soft piano music. Silver service. Great nighttime view of Nairobi's skyline lit up.

Tamarind
National Bank House, Harambee Avenue
Tel: 020-251811/220473
Open Monday–Saturday noon–2.30pm and daily 7pm–12.30am. Chic and lively. One of Nairobi's top restaurants. The best seafood away from the coast. Try the Prawns Piri Piri or any of the crab dishes.

Carnivore
Off Langata Road
Tel: 020-605933-5/602766-9

Right: a typical Kenyan dinner – goat and spinach

Open daily noon–2.30pm and 7pm–midnight. If you ever wanted to know what zebra, giraffe, ostrich, crocodile, impala and other wild meats taste like, this is the place for you. Great haunches of meat are spit-roasted on swords and then carved directly on to your plate. Eat as much as you like. (There's also an *à la carte* and vegetarian menu.) Try a *dawa* (vodka, honey and lime juice) before you start.

The Horseman Restaurant
Karen Shopping Centre
Tel: 020-882033/882782
Choose from five different restaurants offering a range of international cuisine. Opening hours vary.

Pampa Churrascaria
Panari Sky Centre, Mombasa Road
Tel: 020-828132
Open daily for lunch and dinner. A Brazilian restaurant specialising in meats cooked in a range of exciting recipes, with a salad bar reported to be the best in Kenya.

The Talisman Restaurant
320 Ngong Road, Karen
Tel: 020-883213/4
A fusion of Oriental and European dishes. Set in a beautiful garden in Karen. Open for lunch and dinner.

French
Pango Gourmet Brasserie
Fairview Hotel, Bishops Road
Tel: 020-2881000/330
Elegant, cosy lunch and dinner venue with an underground wine bar.

Ibis Restaurant
Norfolk Hotel, Harry Thuku Road
Tel: 020-250900
Open daily 12.30–2pm and 7.30–10pm. The French *nouvelle cuisine* is exquisite. Beautiful surroundings and good service.

Lord Errol Restaurant
Ruaka Road, Runda Estate, off Limuru Road
Tel: 020-7121308/7122433
One of Kenya's finest restaurants. The grand entrance and decor reflect the Happy Valley era of the late 1930s. The cuisine is classical French.

Le Rustique
General Mathenge Drive, off Ring Road, Westlands
Tel: 020-3753081
Situated in a garden setting. Very popular lunchtime venue, plus candlelit dinner every Wednesday. International cuisine. Reasonably priced.

Italian
Mediterraneo Restaurant
The Junction Shopping Centre
Tel: 020-3878608/3873823
Woodvale Grove, Westlands
Tel: 020-4447494/4450349
Probably the most popular Italian restaurants in Kenya, serving classic Italian fare at reasonable prices. Open for both lunch and dinner.

Trattoria
Kaunda/Wabera Street
Tel: 020-340855/240205
Open daily 12.30–2.30pm and 7.30–11pm. A long-time favourite of local Italians and tourists alike.

Chinese
China Plate Restaurant
Chancery Building, Valley Road
Tel: 020-2719194
Good selection of authentic Chinese food. Open for lunch and dinner.

Hong Kong Restaurant
Koinange Street
Tel: 020-228612/341121
Open 12.30–3pm and 6–10.30pm. Closed Mondays. Another old favourite serving good Cantonese food.

Japanese
Akasaka
680 Hotel, Muindi Mbingu Street
Tel: 020-220299
Open daily 12.30–2pm and 6.30–11pm. The best Japanese in town. Try a lunchbox – soup, chicken, sushi, tempura fish or meat with rice, stir-fried vegetables and salad and green tea.

Furusato
Karuna Road (behind the Sarit Centre),
Westlands
Tel: 020-4447089/4442508
Open daily noon–3pm and 7–11pm. This restaurant features a sushi bar (choose any kind of fish from tuna, octopus, salmon, prawns, lobster and more) and four *tepanaki* tables, where the chef cooks food as you eat. Delicious salads.

Pavement Club 'n' Cafe
Westview Centre, Ring Road, Westlands
Tel: 020-4442357/4441711
Restaurant open daily from noon until the last customer leaves. This very popular cafe features a Japanese restaurant with sushi and *tepanaki* tables. The main restaurant serves Thai and Continental dishes. This is a great place for dancing, which starts around 9pm

Indian
Anghiti Restaurant
New Rehema House, Rhapta Road, Westlands
Tel: 020-4442553
Muthaiga Shopping Centre, Limuru Road,
Muthaiga
Tel: 020-3740292
Serves delicate Mughal cuisine. Open for lunch and dinner.

Haandi
The Mall, Uhuru Highway, Westlands
Tel: 020-4448294-5
Open daily 12.30–2.30pm and 7.30–11pm. Reservations are essential at this elegant and very popular Indian restaurant where the food is great and you can watch the chefs through a glass wall.

Thai
Siam Thai Restaurant
Unga House, Westlands
Tel: 020-3751728
Open 12.30–3pm and 6–11pm. Serves genuine Thai dishes. This is the only Thai restaurant in Kenya.

For Breakfast
Dorman's Cafes
The Junction Shopping Centre, Sarit Centre,
Village Market, Muthaiga Shopping Centre

Serve the very best Kenyan coffee, along with a great breakfast, brunch or snack.

Nairobi Java House
Down Town, Adam's Arcade, The Junction Shopping Centre, ABC Shopping Centre and Gigiri
Very popular for breakfasts and lunch, serving their own brand of Kenya coffee. Good quantity and quality servings for your money.

Thorn Tree Cafe
The Sarova Stanley, Kenyatta Avenue/ Kimathi Street
Tel: 020-316377/228830
Open all day, 7am–11pm. Famous pavement cafe attached to the Stanley Hotel. Serves a selection of burgers, steaks, sandwiches, soups and salads, including breakfast.

Mombasa and the Coast
The food in the coast hotels is generally excellent. Most people tend to eat in their hotel and then take advantage of the in-house entertainment provided. The choices up and down the coast are legion – Chinese, Indian, Italian, Continental, African and of course great seafood. Some restaurants are ritzy grill rooms, others have majestic ocean views.

Right: chicken in the Mughal style

Nyali Beach Hotel
Nyali, North Coast, Mombasa
Tel: 041-471551/67
The finest of Kenya's beach hotels has five different restaurants (Italian, Asian/Arabic, African, Seafood and Oriental).

The Tamarind
Cement Cilo Road, Nyali
Tel: 041-474600/1/2
Open daily 11am–3pm and 7–11.30pm. The Tamarind is a must – a Moorish-style restaurant set on a hill overlooking the old harbour and serving superb seafood specialities.

Fort Jesus Sound and Light Show
Jahazi Marine
Tel: 041-5487365
A unique evening that begins with a Dhow Sundowner cruise, followed by a *son et lumière* show and a five-course gourmet meal served *al fresco* within Fort Jesus.

Tamarind Dhow
Cement Cilo Road, Nyali
Tel: 041-474600/1/2

For the ultimate eating experience, dine on a dhow while you cruise around Tudor Creek with fine views of Mombasa's Old Town and Fort Jesus. Great seafood.

Italian
La Veranda Italian Restaurant & Pizzeria
Mwea Tabere Street, behind Nakumatt Nyali Shopping Centre
Tel: 041-5485452
Specialises in homemade pasta, Italian pizzas and seafood dishes. Open for both lunch and dinner.

Indian
Singh's
Mwembe Tayari Road, Mombasa
Tel: 041-2493283
Open noon–2.30pm and 7–10.30pm. Popular restaurant with the locals, serving dishes from northern India.

Shehnai
Fatemi House, Maungano Road, Mombasa
Tel: 041-2222847
Open Tuesday–Sunday noon–2pm and

7–10pm. Serves Mughal *nouvelle cuisine* and tandoori – light north Indian dishes eminently suited to the climate.

Minar
Nyali Golf Club, North Coast
Tel: 041-471220/472443
Open for breakfast, lunch, tea and dinner 8am–11pm. Serves exotic and delicate Mughal cuisine, much the same as its namesake in Nairobi.

Chinese
Hong Kong Restaurant
Malindi Road, North Coast Mombasa
Tel: 041-5485422
Open 12.30–3pm and 6–10.30pm. Closed Mondays. Another old favourite serving good Cantonese food – just like its namesake in Nairobi.

North of Mombasa
Hemingways
Watamu
Tel: 042-32624/32276
The best hotel in this popular beach resort has an excellent seafood buffet lunch on Sunday and their restaurant is worth visiting any day of the week.

Driftwood Beach Club
Silversands, Malindi
Tel: 042-20155/30569
Temporary membership of the club entitles you to use the swimming pool, the bar or the very popular restaurant, with delicious seafood, a good buffet and an excellent Sunday curry.

Barbecue Grill
Peponi Hotel, Lamu
Tel: 0734-203082/0722-203082
The one upmarket hotel in laid-back Swahili Lamu (and one of the few places in town with a liquor licence) offers excellent food and a few imaginative surprises within its calm interior.

Old Man and the Sea Restaurant
Seafront, Malindi
Tel: 042-31106
Small restaurant serving freshly caught seafood. Very good value.

NIGHTLIFE

Don't come to Kenya if you're a party animal. On safari you'll be in bed by 10pm so that you can get up at the crack of dawn. In Nairobi, a good night out means dinner and perhaps a few spins at the casino.

Nairobi Restaurants/Hotels
The **Carnivore** restaurant, off Langata Road, has nightly entertainment in its Simba Saloon: rock music every Wednesday, Mega Cultural night including MTV, Swing and Mulembe on Friday (with African food and drink), Simba Disco Inferno (usually live) on Saturday and a soul disco on Sunday.

The **Safari Park Hotel** complex, which is located on the Thika Road, is home to six restaurants (African, Japanese, Chinese, Italian, Indian and Continental food), one of which, the African-style Nyama Choma Ranch, puts on a nightly floor show by the Safari Cats – dancers combining modern and traditional African dance, with marvellous costumes.

Discos
There are a number of bars with small discos in and around town. The **Pavement Club 'n' Cafe** in the Westview Centre, Westlands, has dancing on Wednesday, Friday, Saturday and Sunday. There's dancing too at **Gypsy's**, a tapas bar in Westlands, **Zanze Bar** in the Kenya Cinema Plaza, **Outside Inn** on Karen Road in Karen, and a few others that operate on Friday and Saturday nights only. Other nightspots include the **Florida Night Club**, on Koinange Street, featuring disco music in smoke-filled rooms.

Left: the terrace of the Tamarind restaurant, Mombasa
Above: advertising at a Mombasa bar

Casinos

Nairobi has a number of casinos, the best known being the **International Casino** (Museum Hill, Westlands Road), followed by **Mayfair Casino Club** at the Holiday Inn Mayfair Court (Parklands Road, Westlands), the **Four Aces Casino** (Waiyaki Way, Westlands) and the casinos at the **Hotel Intercontinental** and the **Grand Regency** in the city centre.

Theatre and Cinema

The **National Theatre**, **Phoenix Players**, **Braeburn Theatre** and the **French**, **Italian** and **German Cultural Centres** all offer good-quality classical, traditional and contemporary stage productions and musical entertainment.

There are 14 cinemas in Nairobi, including two drive-ins and seven cineplexes – **Fox Theatres** (Down Town), **Kenya Cinema** (Moi Avenue), **20th Century Plaza** (Mama Ngina Street), **Sarit Centre** (Westlands), **Nu Metro Cinemas** (Village Market, Prestige Plaza and The Junction Shopping Centre) and **Dream Theatres** (Panari Sky Centre) – which show the latest films. Check the daily newspapers or the *Going Out Guide* or *Going Places* guide for listings.

Nightlife on the Coast

Nearly all hotels offer evening entertainment for their guests such as fire-eaters, jugglers, dancing (Samburu or Maasai) and snake-charmers, with middle-of-the-road discos on Friday and Saturday nights. In Nyali, just over the Nyali Bridge, there is Nyali Cinemax with a movie theatre, bowling alley, casino and restaurants.

Severin Sea Lodge *(see page 58)* offers sundowners and light music on an early-evening dhow trip that takes you to Fort Jesus for lavish *son e lumière* entertainment depicting the history of the coast, followed by a banquet within the fort. **Tamarind Dhow** *(see page 57)* serves up the dhow trip and a meal afloat, without the historical spectacular.

There are a large number of discos to choose from in the many hotels on **Diani Beach**, as well as a couple of casinos, and a variety of restaurants along the Diani Beach Road.

Malindi offers the **Star Dust** nightclub and the **Malindi Casino**, both located in the centre of town.

Above: exuberant floor show at the Carnivore in Nairobi

CALENDAR OF EVENTS

January

Hog Charge (bicycle cross-country)
Fishing competitions in Mtwapa and Kilifi
Mid-Jan – Ladies Kennel Association Dog Show, Nairobi

February

10 to 4 Mountain Bike Challenge, Mt Kenya
Mid-Feb – International Billfish Tournament, Malindi

March

Early Mar – Watamu Sea Fishing Club Festival
KBC Safari Rally
Kenya Open Golf Championship, Nairobi,
Broadbill Competition, Watamu
East African Kennel Club Dog Show, Nairobi

April

Easter Frolic fishing competition, Kilifi and Mtwapa
Kenya Derby, Ngong Road Racecourse
Easter Horse Show, Nairobi

May

Mombasa International Marathon
Motor Rally, Western Kenya Motorsports Club

June

Early June – Rhino Charge (off-road endurance event)
Motor Rally, Rift Valley Motor & Sports Club
Kenya St Leger, Ngong Road Racecourse
Mid-June – Agricultural Society of Kenya, Nakuru Show
North Kenya Polo Tournament, Timau
Last weekend – International Tusker Safari Sevens (seven-a-side rugby)

July

Maralal International Camel Derby
Nairobi Polo Tournament, Nairobi
Kabete Happening Horse Show, Nairobi
Timau Horse Show, Timau
Silverdale Horse Show, Nairobi

August

Motor Rally, Kenya Motorsports Club

Laikipia Camel Derby, Rumuruti
Mugs' Mug Polo Tournament, Nairobi
Horse of the Year Show, Nairobi
Agricultural Society of Kenya, Mombasa Show
Maulidi (Prophet's birthday) on Lamu

September

Early-Sept – Enterprise and Mwamba rugby knockout cups (regional East African tournaments)
Concours d'Elegance (cars and motorcycles), Nairobi
North Kenya Bank Tournament, Watamu
International Polo Tournament, Nairobi
Horse racing season starts (until July)
Kenya Horticultural Society Flower Show, Nairobi
End-Sept – Agricultural Society of Kenya, Nairobi Show

October

Churchill/Morson Light Tackle, Malindi
Football, Moi Golden Cup Final, Nairobi
Kenyatta Cup, Ngong Road Racecourse
End Oct – East African Kennel Club Dog Show, Nairobi

November

Motor Rally, Kisumu
East African Safari Classic Rally
Matthews/Devilliers Memorial Fishing Tournament, Malindi
Manyatta Polo Tournament, Gilgil
Sanctuary Farm Horse Show, Naivasha
Mid/End November – Christmas Craft Fair

December

Pemba Channel Fishing Club Billfish Tournament, Shimoni
Uhuru Cup, Ngong Road Racecourse
Christmas Pantomimes in Nairobi (check newspapers for dates)
Kilifi Christmas Competition
26 Dec – Boxing Day races at Ngong Racecourse

There are a number of exhibitions, cultural and sporting events throughout the year that don't necessarily take place every year. Consult the daily newspapers or the *Going Out Guide* or *Going Places* guide to find out what's happening, when and where.

Practical
Information

GETTING THERE

By Air

There are two international airports: Jomo Kenyatta International Airport (JKIA) in Nairobi, 16km (10 miles) from the city centre, and Moi International Airport in Mombasa. The two airports are linked by domestic flights.

By Sea and Train

Regular ship passenger sevices to Mombasa were suspended in the 1970s. Few cargo ships offer passenger berths, and cruise liners only make occasional calls. No direct access from abroad is possible by rail.

Short cruises are available on the *Royal Star* from Mombasa or Zanzibar (book through Maniago Travel & Cruises, 1st floor, ABC Place, Waiyaki Way, Nairobi, tel: 020-4449461/2, email: info@maniagotrvl.com; 1st floor, Nakumatt Centre, Bamburi Road, Mombasa, tel: 041-5486762/3, email: mombasa@maniagotrvl.com.

By Road

Road transit through northeast and northwest Africa is uncertain. Overland safari companies still do it and fly over difficult areas – but the journey is long and hard.

There are roads in from Somalia, Ethiopia, Tanzania and Uganda but the only safe routes by road would be from Tanzania and Uganda, and then only for the real adventurers – and never at night.

TRAVEL ESSENTIALS

Visas and Travel Documents

All visitors must have a valid passport. A visa is required by everyone except most Commmonwealth citizens. You can apply for one from any Kenyan Embassy or Consulate, or from a British Embassy in countries where Kenya has no diplomatic representation. Alternatively, you can get one at the airport when you arrive, but expect queues; in this case, ensure you take Sterling or dollars with you. The fee for a single entry visa, valid for three months is £35 or US$50. A multiple-entry visa (US$100) is valid for one year, and a transit visa (US$20) for seven days.

If you intend to hire a vehicle while in Kenya, bring your domestic or international driving licence. For visitors from the UK, an international driving permit is recommended (available from the AA, the RAC and some Post Offices).

Vaccinations and Health Precautions

Yellow fever vaccinations are recommended at least 10 days before travelling and a yellow fever vaccination certificate is mandatory. It's also advisable to take precautions against typhoid, hepatitis A, tetanus and polio.

Malaria is endemic below altitudes of 1,800m (6,000ft). Begin taking a course of prophylactics recommended by your doctor two weeks before travelling, and continue taking them throughout your stay and for two weeks after your return home. Better still, avoid getting bitten. Mosquitoes bite mainly at dusk and during the night and you're particularly at risk in game parks and on the coast. Use insect repellant (varieties with a high level of DEET are recommended) liberally and wear long sleeves, trousers and socks after sundown. Sleep under a mosquito net or in an air-conditioned room if possible. If you develop flu-like symptoms within six weeks of arriving

Left: coastal transport, old style
Right: safari transport, new style

home, you should insist on being tested for malaria, preferably at your nearest tropical diseases hospital.

Customs

Visitors can bring in 200 cigarettes or 250g of tobacco or 50 cigars, 1 litre of alcohol and 1 litre of perfume, duty free.

Climate

The equatorial sun is deceptively intense, so protective sun-cream and a hat are absolutely essential. Heat stroke combined with the high altitude can be particularly unpleasant so avoid rushing around in the midday sun.

There are two rainy seasons – the long rains from the end of March to early May and the short rains from mid-October to mid-December – but in recent years global climate change has made both seasons unpredictable. When it does come, much of the rain falls from late afternoon through the night, often with sunny mornings.

The dry season is from early January to the end of March. The cool dry season is mid-June to early September.

Coastal areas remain hot all year round, though slightly cooler in July and August. Higher land areas can be warm during the day but quite cool at night.

Clothing

Bring loose-fitting cotton clothes with a light woollen sweater or jacket for warmth in the evenings. Comfortable walking shoes are essential. Dress in Kenya is casual, but scanty or provocative clothing may cause offence so use your common sense and tact, particularly in areas with a high Muslim population. Topless sunbathing and nudity are not allowed anywhere.

Electricity

The standard supply is 240 volts (50 cycles AC). Bring a small step-down voltage converter for any 110-volt appliances. Tourist hotels and safari camps or lodges usually have their own generators.

Time

Kenya is three hours ahead of Greenwich Mean Time (UTC). Daylight is an almost constant 12 hours, 6.30am–6.30pm.

GETTING ACQUAINTED

When to Visit

To see the wildebeest migration in the Maasai Mara, come in July/August. But Kenya is beautiful at any time of year.

Geography

Straddling the equator, Kenya's 582,644 sq km (224,960 sq miles) include almost every type of geographic landform, from a snow-capped mountain to true desert.

Bound on three sides by Ethiopia, Sudan, Somalia, Uganda and Tanzania, her 483km (300 miles) of tropical coastline fringe the Indian Ocean, with a coral reef running the length of the coast that is a marine Eden – much of it protected as marine national parks.

Kenya's capital Nairobi is in the south of the country at an altitude of 1,670m (5,479ft). The population of Nairobi is approaching 2.5 million.

Government and Economy

The presidential and legislative elections held in December 2002 were a marked turning point in Kenyan politics. Mwai Kibaki and the National Rainbow Coalition (NARC) won a landslide victory, pushing the Kenya African National Union (KANU) into opposition, ending Daniel Arap Moi's 24-year reign, and giving Kenya a new ruling party for the first time since Independence in 1963.

Kenya is still one of the most prosperous countries in black Africa. Tourism is now the

Left: various styles of traditional dress in Lamu

biggest source of foreign revenue, surpassing tea, coffee and horticultural exports.

Population Mix

There are more than 40 different ethnic groups in Kenya, many with their own languages, but English is the official language and Kiswahili the national language. In urban areas, most people speak English or Kiswahili and their own tribal language.

Kenya's population is estimated to be around 32 million and is increasing by just over 2 percent annually.

Religion

About 70 percent of Kenyans are Christian (Anglican, Baptist, Coptic, Catholic, Orthodox, Pentecostal and Presbyterian) with numerous Afro-Christian sects. Twenty percent of the population are Islamic and approximately 10 percent are Sikhs and Hindus.

How Not to Offend

Kenyans are very polite, friendly and hospitable. Greetings are important and no conversation begins without first saying *Jambo* (Kiswahili for 'Hello') or *Habari gani?* ('How are things?'). Unknown men should be addressed as *Bwana*, or *Mzee* for older men. Women should be addressed as *Mama*.

Petting in public is frowned upon. Men often hold hands in friendship, but you rarely see anyone behaving more intimately than this in public. Nude or topless bathing is not allowed.

MONEY MATTERS

Kenyan currency is the shilling (Ksh), divided into 100 cents with nickel coins of 20, 10 and 5 shillings and 50 cents, and copper coins of 1 shilling. Notes are in denominations of 1,000, 500, 200, 100, 50 and 20 shillings. One Kenyan pound is 20 shillings. One 'bob' is one shilling.

Following recent devaluations, exchange rates are fluctuating dramatically, so check with different banks before changing your money. You can change money at banks, hotels or one of dozens of bureaux de change. There is no point in black-market dealing

as you won't get a better rate. It's safest to bring traveller's cheques rather than large amounts of cash.

There are no longer any currency restrictions for visitors, and you can take as much money as you want into and out of Kenya. But it is unwise to take away large amounts in Kenyan shillings, as you may have a problem exchanging them abroad.

Credit Cards

Visa, MasterCard, American Express and Diners are accepted in many outlets. Look out for the 'Pesa Point' ATM network around the country that accepts almost any credit card, including Visa.

Be sure to ask for the payment voucher to be filled out in front of you, particularly in restaurants and petrol stations, and at the duty-free shop at the airport – there have been many incidents of fraudulent transactions made with faked signatures.

Tipping

In restaurants, it is usual to round your bill up to the nearest 100 shillings, even where the service charge is included (it's the only way to be sure that your waiter will receive the money). In private houses it is usual for guests to club together to tip 100 shillings per person, per day. Please don't forget to tip gardeners and *askaris* (guards) as their con-

---

Above: cash dispensers are increasingly common in Nairobi and coastal resorts

tribution to making your stay enjoyable is just as important as the more visible cooks and house servants. Car park attendants, supermarket porters and similar personnel can be tipped 20 shillings.

Banking Hours

Banks are open Monday to Friday 9am–3pm, and on the first and last Saturday of each month 9–11am. Outside these hours money can be changed in hotels or bureaux de change, or at the 24-hour bank at Jomo Kenyatta Airport.

GETTING AROUND

Public Transport

Travelling by *matatu* (brightly painted public minibuses) is a dangerous business. Like larger buses and coaches, they frequently overturn, often in rivers, killing or maiming many passengers. Even on good days, they are driven much too quickly and are regularly involved in near-misses and minor accidents. Use this form of public transport only if you are fully insured and prepared to risk the consequences.

For a reliable bus service to or from Mombasa, contact Coastline Safaris; tel: 020-217592/245190; or in Mombasa, tel: 041-2312083/2220158; and Wakamba Pub-

lic Road Services; tel: 020-223304/556062, 0722-203753.

Taxis

Always use a taxi at night unless you're familiar with the town centres. The roads are riddled with potentially lethal potholes and are very badly lit. Negotiate the fare before you jump in or you could find yourself grossly overcharged. Reliable companies, with set fares per kilometre, are Kenatco (tel: 02-225123/824248 in Nairobi or 041-2227503/ 2313402 in Mombasa) and Jatco Taxis in Nairobi, tel: 020-4448162/ 0722648383.

Car Hire

Hiring your own vehicle can provide one the best ways to see Kenya, although extreme care must be taken. If you're worried about driving on unknown roads, hire a driver too – it costs an extra Kshs 1,500–2,500 per day and saves worrying about leaving your valuables unattended or parking in town centres. He will also be able to tell you everything you want to know about Kenyan politics, wildlife etc.

For most game parks and off-road driving, hire a four-wheel-drive vehicle, especially in the rainy season. A Suzuki is adequate for two people although you may find it claustrophobic for more than this. Range Rovers, Land-Rovers, Pajeros, Nissan Patrols etc, are also readily available.

Above: rising over the Maasai Mara

A saloon car will do for driving around town. At the coast an open-topped car is good for short trips but a more solid vehicle is advisable for longer distances or if you plan to leave luggage unattended.

Avis, Hertz and Budget all have outlets in Kenya but you'll generally find better value for money at the smaller car-hire companies *(see below)*. Try to reserve your vehicle well in advance.

If the companies listed below can't help you, browse through the tourist literature on your first day in Kenya to see what special week-long, weekend or unlimited-mileage rates are on offer elsewhere. Or check www.magicalkenya.com (the official website for the Kenya Tourist Board).

Always ask to see the vehicle before you pay or you could find yourself with an old banger that hasn't been serviced for years and will let you down miles from help. Make sure that you have a spare tyre and the necessary tools to change it. Also be sure you have a key to unlock wheel-locks, too.

Check what you should do in the event of a breakdown. Some companies expect you to repair the vehicle and get back to Nairobi under your own steam, where they will reimburse your costs (keep the receipts). Others may come and help you.

Most companies stipulate that drivers must be over 23 years of age and in possession of a valid national or international driving licence. You can't hire a car without taking out third party insurance at the same time. It is also sensible to take out Collision Damage Waiver (CDW) so that if you damage your own or another vehicle you are not liable to pay costs. Rates for CDW vary so check with individual companies.

Car-Hire Companies
• Nairobi
Concorde Car Hire, tel: 020-4448953; fax: 020-4448135; email: carhire@concorde.co.ke
Budget Rent A Car, tel: 020-223581/ 822370; www.budget-kenya.com.
Several other car-hire companies have desks at the airport.

• Mombasa
Budget Rent A Car, tel: 041-2221281/ 2490034; www.budget-kenya.com.

Payless Car Hire and Tours, tel: 041-2221281/3434887

Parking
Car thefts are on the increase, even in daylight in the city centre. Try to park in private parking areas when possible (the Intercontinental Hotel in Nairobi, for instance, has high-rise parking at Ksh100 an hour). All-day parking on central Nairobi's main streets currently costs Ksh70.

Wherever you park, you will usually find a youth willing to watch your vehicle while you are away, for which you should tip him Ksh20 on your return.

Trains
The main railway line runs from Mombasa on the coast to Kisumu in the west. The train service is slow but surprisingly reliable and very cheap. One overnight train runs each day between Mombasa and Nairobi, leaving both stations promptly at 7pm and arriving at 8am. Trains run from Nairobi to Mombasa on Monday, Wednesday, Friday, and the other way on Tuesday, Thursday and Sunday.

The old-fashioned sleepers and dining car were once reminiscent of the old-world elegance of the original settlers. Sadly, today it's all a bit shabby but it's still a relaxing and enjoyable way to travel, at least in one direction. Reserve your tickets well in advance from Nairobi or Mombasa station (tel: Nairobi 020-221211, Mombasa 041-2312220; www.eastafricashuttles.com/ train.htm).

Right: overland travellers should be prepared for every eventuality

Wildlife Checklist

Mammal	Where found
African wild cat	Widely distributed.
Antelope: sable	Shimba Hills. Rare.
Antelope: roan	Maasai Mara, Shimba Hills. Quite rare.
Baboon	Aberdares, Nairobi Park, Amboseli, Samburu, Tsavo. Widespread.
Bat-eared fox	Amboseli, Nairobi Park. Nocturnal.
Bongo	Aberdares, Mount Kenya.
Buffalo	Tsavo, Samburu, Amboseli, Maasai Mara. Widely distributed.
Bush pig	Forests and bushland. Rarely seen. Nocturnal.
Bushbaby	Forests and bushland. Widely distributed, but nocturnal.
Bushbuck	Dense bushlands in the southern half of Kenya. Mainly nocturnal.
Cheetah	Nairobi Park, Amboseli, Samburu, Maasai Mara. Grasslands.
Dik-dik	Tsavo, Amboseli, Maasai Mara, Samburu. Dry bush country.
Duiker	Forests, dense bushlands, high grass. Rare.
Eland	Nairobi Park, Tsavo, Maasai Mara. Grasslands, mountain moorlands.
Elephant	Aberdares, Tsavo, Maasai Mara, Mount Kenya, Amboseli, Samburu.
Gazelle: Thomson's	Amboseli, Nairobi Park, Maasai Mara. Grasslands and savannah.
Gazelle: Grant's	Tsavo, Nairobi Park, Amboseli, Maasai Mara, Samburu. Grasslands and savannah.
Genet (various)	Often seen at camps and lodges. Nocturnal.
Gerenuk	Tsavo, Samburu, Amboseli, Lake Magadi. Dry bush.
Giant forest hog	Aberdares, Mount Kenya. Forests.
Giraffe: Maasai	Tsavo, Nairobi Park, Maasai Mara, Amboseli, southern Kenya.
Giraffe: Reticulated	Samburu, northern Kenya.
Giraffe: Rothschild's	Nakuru.
Hartebeest	Open grasslands.
Hippopotamus	Maasai Mara, Tsavo, Amboseli. Rivers, swamps and lakes.
Honey badger	Often seen near camps and lodges. Nocturnal.
Hunting dog	Tsavo, Maasai Mara, Samburu. Very rare.
Hyrax: rock	Nairobi Park. Widespread.
Hyrax: tree	Forests. Nocturnal.
Impala	Tsavo, Nairobi Park, Amboseli, Maasai Mara, Samburu. Widespread.
Jackal: black- or silver-backed	Amboseli, Nairobi Park, Maasai Mara. Grasslands.
Klipspringer	Bogoria, Naivasha.
Kudu: greater	Shimba Hills, Bogoria and Samburu. Rare.
Kudu: lesser	Tsavo, Amboseli, northern Kenya.
Leopard	All parks. Secretive.
Lion	Nairobi Park, Maasai Mara, Tsavo, Amboseli, Samburu. Grasslands, open bushlands, semi-desert.
Mongoose (various)	Widely distributed.
Monkey: black and white colobus	Mount Kenya, Nakuru, Aberdares, Naivasha. Highland forests and Diani Beach.
Monkey: red colobus	Arabuko-Sokoke forest.
Monkey: Sykes'	Widely distributed.
Monkey: vervet	Widely distributed.
Oribi	Grasslands, open woodlands. Very rare.
Oryx: Beisa	Samburu, northern Kenya.
Oryx: fringe-eared	Tsavo, Amboseli.
Otter	Widely distributed – lakes, rivers etc.

Reedbuck: Bohor	Nairobi Park, Nakuru. Grasslands with bushes.
Reedbuck: Chanler's mountain	Nairobi Park. Rocky slopes and escarpments.
Rhinoceros: black	Tsavo, Nairobi Park, Amboseli, Maasai Mara, Mount Kenya, Aberdares, Nakuru.
Rhinoceros: white	Nakuru, Solio Ranch.
Serval cat	Widely distributed but rarely seen.
Spotted hyena	Widely distributed.
Steinbok	Grasslands.
Suni	Highland and coastal forests, dense bushlands.
Topi	Maasai Mara.
Warthog	Savannah and bushy grasslands. Everywhere.
Waterbuck	Tsavo, Amboseli, Nairobi Park, Samburu.
Waterbuck: Defassa	Tsavo, Amboseli, Nairobi Park, Nakuru.
Wildebeest	Maasai Mara, southern Kenya, Amboseli.
Zebra: Burchell's	Maasai Mara, Amboseli. Open grasslands.
Zebra: Grevy's	Samburu, northern Kenya.

Bird Checklist

African spoonbill	Rift Valley lakes, lagoons and dams.
Barbet	Many species.
Barbet: red and yellow	Tsavo, Samburu. Dry termite mounds.
Barbet: D'Arnaud's	Widespread.
Bee-eater: carmine	Coastal areas.
Bee-eater: cinnamon-chested	Mount Kenya, Highlands.
Bee-eater: little	Widely distributed.
Bee-eater: white-fronted	Rift Valley.
Black crake	Walking on hippo's back. Marshes, swamps, lakes and river shores.
Bustard: black-bellied	Maasai Mara, Tsavo, Amboseli. Cultivated areas and open grasslands.
Bustard: kori	Nairobi Park, Amboseli, Tsavo, Samburu, Maasai Mara. Open savannah and thorn bush.
Buzzard: augur	Mountains, savannah, cultivated areas.
Cormorant	Naivasha and Nakuru.
Courser	Dry bush country and shorelines.
Crowned crane	Widely distributed.
Doves	Many species, widely distributed.
Eagle: African fish	Along rivers, lakes, etc.
Eagle: Bateleur	Open savannah and thornbush country.
Eagle: martial	Nairobi Park. Widely distributed.
Eagle: tawny	Widely distributed.
Eagle: Verreaux's	Nairobi Park. Rocky hills, mountains.
Egret: cattle	Widely distributed, often with grazing flocks.
Egret: yellow-billed	Swamps, rivers, lakes.
Falcon	Many species.
Finches	Widely distributed.
Flamingo: greater	Lakes Magadi and Nakuru.
Flamingo: lesser	Lakes Magadi, Bogoria and Nakuru.
Francolin	Widespread
Francolin: Jackson's	Aberdares, Mount Kenya. Mountain forests.
Geese: Egyptian	Widely distributed.
Geese: knob-billed	Lake Naivasha. Lakes, pools and wooded swamps.
Geese: spurwing	Lakes and rivers.
Go-away bird: white-bellied	Widespread.
Goshawk: pale chanting	Acacia and bush country.
Guineafowl: helmeted	Widely distributed.
Guineafowl: vulturine	Samburu. Dry bush. Northern Kenya, Tsavo.
Gull	Inland waters and at coast.
Hawk	Several species.
Heron: night	Naivasha and Nakuru.
Heron: Goliath	Lake Naivasha. Never far from water.
Heron: black-headed	Common, usually near water.
Honey guide	Indicate location of bee's nest.

Hoopoe	Woodland and riverine forest.
Hornbill	Widely distributed.
Hornbill: ground	Savannah. Forages on ground.
Ibis	Widely distributed.
Jacana (lily trotter)	Naivasha, Amboseli.
Kingfisher	Many species. Usually near water.
Kite: yellow-billed	Savannah, lakes, rivers, towns.
Kite: black-shouldered	Grasslands and cultivated areas.
Mousebird	Forest edges, bushy savannah, scrub and cultivated areas.
Nightjar	Many species. Distinctive call.
Ostrich: Somali	Samburu, north-eastern Kenya.
Ostrich: common	Widely distributed in grasslands.
Owl: Verreaux's eagle	Acacia trees in riverine forest or savannah.
Owl: African marsh	Nairobi Park, Mt Kenya and Rift Valley.
Oxpecker: red/yellow-billed	On animal's backs. Widespread.
Parrot: red-headed	Mountain forests.
Pelican	Naivasha and Nakuru. Inland lakes.
Pigeons	Many species, widely distributed.
Plover	Many species. Samburu, Lake Magadi. Swamps, mudflats, grasslands, lakes, rivers, dams etc.
Purple gallinule	Naivasha. Swamps and papyrus marshes.
Red-crested coot	Rift Valley. Lakes, dams and swamps.
Roller: broad-billed	Forests, savannah, riverine forests and mountain areas.
Roller: lilac-breasted	Savannah and dry bush.
Sand grouse	Several species, widely distributed.
Secretary bird	Grasslands and light bush country.
Shrike: fiscal	Ubiquitous.
Starling: superb	Lodges and picnic sites. Common.

Starling: golden-breasted	Tsavo, Samburu.
Stork: Abdim's	Comes in from Sudan in large flocks.
Stork: hammerkop	Rivers, pools, shallow lake shores.
Stork: marabou	Widely distributed.
Stork: open-billed	Lakes, marshes and large lagoons.
Stork: saddle-billed	Amboseli, Maasai Mara, Buffalo Springs. Swamps, marshes and reedy lake shores.
Stork: yellow-billed	Widely distributed near water.
Sunbirds	Many species.
Trogon: Narina's	Highland and mountain forest.
Turaco: Fischer's	Coastal highland and mountain forest.
Vultures	Many species and widely distributed, particularly near kills.
Weavers	Many species.
Woodpecker	Many species.
Wydah birds	Many species.

Reptiles and others

Black mamba	Rare.
Chameleon: horned	Widespread.
Dung beetle	Everywhere but especially Tsavo area.
Giant millipede	Tree trunks and fallen leaves. Undergrowth.
Green tree snake	Slithering along tree branches.
Lizard: Nile monitor	Rivers.
Lizard: Agama	Lodges and camps. Rocky outcrops (males blue with red heads).
Lizard: spotted monitor	Savannah and dry bush.
Nile crocodile	Tsavo, Samburu, Shaba, Maasai Mara, Nairobi Park. Rivers and lakes.
Puff adder	Bush and scrub. Widespread.
Rock python	Widely distributed but rarely seen.
Scorpions	Hot, dry bush.
Spitting cobra	Widespread.
Tortoise	Savannah and grasslands.
Turtle	Sea, streams and rivers.

Planes

Kenya Airways operates regular flights between Nairobi, Mombasa, Malindi and Lamu (tel: Nairobi 020-3274747; Mombasa 041-2125000; Malindi 042-20237; Lamu 042-632040/633155). **Air Kenya** operates regular flights between Nairobi and Malindi, and to the Maasai Mara, Amboseli, Tsavo, Kiwayu, Lamu and Samburu from Wilson Airport on Langata Road, Nairobi (tel: 020-605745/606539; www.airkenya.com).

SafariLink has daily flights to major tourist destinations (tel: 020-600777; www.safarilink-kenya.com).

To destinations around northern Kenya from Nanyuki or Nairobi, including scenic flights, call **Tropic Air**, Nanyuki (tel: 062-32890/1; www.tropicairkenya.com).

Flights to coastal destinations contact **Mombasa Air Safari** (tel: 041-433061/434487; www.mombasaairsafari.com).

You can charter your own single or twin-engine plane to fly anywhere in Kenya from Wilson Airport. Contact **Safari Air Services** (tel: Nairobi 020-3762706) or **Boskovic Air Charters** (tel: 020-606364/606432; www.boskovicaircharters.com). It's not as expensive as you might think.

There are luggage restrictions of 10–15kg (22–33lb) per person on light aircraft.

WILDLIFE

Kenya is known for its game parks (see page 16 for discussion of the parks' purposes and problems). The following are referred to in the Wildlife Checklist: Aberdare National Park, Amboseli National Park, Buffalo Springs National Reserve, Lake Bogoria National Reserve, Lake Nakuru National Park, Maasai Mara National Reserve, Nairobi National Park, Samburu National Reserve, Shaba National Reserve, Tsavo East and Tsavo West National Parks. National Parks are controlled by the Kenya Wildlife Service (KWS), a government body. National Reserves are controlled by the local county councils.

The KWS has introduced an electronic ticketing system for six of its major national parks: Nairobi, Lake Nakuru, Aberdare, Amboseli, Tsavo East and West. The smartcard, available from an office located at the en-

trance of Nairobi National Park, can be paid for in Kenya shillings or US dollars. There are three types of visitor cards: citizen, resident and non-resident. If you produce this card at the point of entry to one of the six parks, the entry fee will be deducted from the credit on your card. If your tour has been organised by a tour operator, the park fees should be included in the total cost of your safari.

If you are visiting/staying in the Maasai Mara Reserve, Mara Triangle and/or conservancies surrounding the Maasai Mara, be sure that you pay all required entry fees before leaving Nairobi. Ask your travel/tour agent about this when making your bookings.

The best times to spot game are at dawn and dusk when most animals feed, and the ideal time to take photographs or videos is early morning or late afternoon. Detailed maps of the parks are readily available.

The Wildlife Checklist includes mammals, birds and some insects and reptiles. It is not comprehensive, but is a good guide to what to look out for and where.

COMMUNICATIONS

Post

Kenyan post is cheap and relatively efficient. The main post office in Nairobi is opposite City Square on Haile Selassie Avenue. It's open Monday–Friday 8am–5pm, Saturday 9am–noon. There are also branches on Moi Avenue and Tom Mboya Street and in shopping centres such as Westlands, Karen, Muthaiga and Village Market.

In Mombasa, the main post office is on Digo Road between Makadera Road and Gusii Street. Many hotels, souvenir shops and stationers also sell stamps.

Above: the famous Carnivore restaurant ventures into cyberspace

Telephones, Faxes, Email etc

Kenya has an excellent communications system for both internal and international services. Direct dialling is possible between most centres in the country, and a full international STD system has been introduced. Unfortunately, the phone service is sometimes unreliable, especially during the rainy season.

Telkom Calling Cards are available in denominations from Ksh100 to Ksh2,000, and can be used for local, trunk or international calls from any telephone. These are available from Telkom Kenya, post offices and authorised dealers. Ask at the post office or your hotel reception.

Local and long-distance calls can be made from public phone boxes, if you can find one that is working. Place the coins ready in the slot before dialling – they will fall through automatically when the telephone is answered – or use a Calling Card.

In major centres around the country, Telkom have introduced TeleCentres with payphone services, internet/email facilities, fax and international calling facilities. Recently introduced is VoIP service for international calls, thus making charges even cheaper. You can also use hotel facilities but they are always much more expensive.

In Mombasa, you can make international calls from the post office on Digo Road.

There are many places in Nairobi and on the coast where you can send email or browse the Internet. Ask for details at your hotel's reception.

There are two major mobile phone (cellphone) networks in Kenya – Safaricom and Celtel – with reception in the major urban areas and the coastal strip. Pay-as-you-go SIM cards are available everywhere in a number of denominations. Both companies offer reciprocating roaming services with many countries.

Useful telephone numbers

Country code for Kenya	254
Code for Nairobi	020
Code for Mombasa	041
Operator	900
Directory enquiries	991
International operator	0195/0196
Fire, police, ambulance	999
VoIP Service	888

Media

There are three English-language daily newspapers in Kenya – the *Nation* (the best), the *Standard* and the *Kenya Times* – as well as the weekly *East African*, which covers the whole East Africa region. Foreign newspapers and magazines including *Time*, *Newsweek* and *The Economist* are sold by street-sellers and also in larger hotels and in shopping malls.

TV channels are shared between the Kenya Broadcasting Corporation (KBC), Kenya Television Network (KTN), Nation, Citizen, Stella and Metro, with CNN interchanging with KTN and Nation. Stella TV carries a variety of programmes, including Sky News, CBS News and coverage of international sporting events. DSTV is offered in a number hotels and restaurants, broadcasting a range of news, sport and films.

As well as KBC's broadcasts in English and Kiswahili, there are several private FM radio stations, including Capital FM, BBC, KBC Radio, Family FM and other local language stations.

HOURS & HOLIDAYS

Business Hours

Offices and shops are open Monday–Friday 8am–5.30pm with an hour's break for lunch around 1pm. Saturday hours are 8am–12.30pm. Small *dukas* (general stores) stay open much later. Many Nairobi shopping centres now open on Sunday. At the coast trade may start as early as 7am but will be interrupted for a long siesta between 12.30 and 4pm; it then resumes until dark.

National Holidays

1 January	New Year's Day
March/April	Good Friday, Easter Monday
1 May	Labour Day
1 June	Madaraka Day (anniversary of self-government)
20 October	Kenyatta Day (anniversary of Jomo Kenyatta's arrest and State of Emergency)
12 December	Jamhuri (Independence) Day
25 December	Christmas Day
26 December	Boxing Day
variable	Idd ul Fitr (Muslim holiday)

ACCOMMODATION

In the list of hotels which follows, $ = under US$100 for a double, $$ = $100–300 and $$$ = over $300.

Nairobi

The best hotels are all outside the town centre, but it's well worth travelling the extra distance to stay in them.

Fairview Hotel
Bishops Road, Nairobi Hill
Tel: 020-2711321/2710090
www.fairviewkenya.com
A delightful hotel only 5 minutes from the town centre. Popular with business travellers. Gift shop and business centre. $$

Grand Regency Hotel
Uhuru Highway
Tel: 020-211199
www.grandregency.co.ke
Just 5 minutes' walk from the central shopping and business area. Several restaurants plus a pool and conference facilities. $$

Holiday Inn Nairobi
Parklands Road, Westlands
PO Box 66807, Nairobi.
Tel: 020-3740920/1
Email: admin@holidayinn.co.ke
A few minutes' drive from Westlands Shopping Centre; 3 conference centres, 2 restaurants, health club, 2 pools, hair salon, boutique, casino, courtesy bus. $$

Jacaranda Hotel
Waiyaki Way, Westlands
Tel: 020-4448713-7
www.jacarandahotels.com
Right next door to the Sarit Centre. Pool, hair salon, shop, business centre, conference centre. $$

The Kentmere Club
Old Limuru Road, Karuri
PO Box 39508, Nairobi
Tel: 066-50625
The best value of all. English-style country inn in beautiful gardens 30 minutes from town. One of the best restaurants in Kenya.

Right: lunch is served in the Norfolk Hotel

Golf, swimming, tennis and squash at nearby Limuru Club. $$

Kenya Comfort Hotel
Corner Muindi Mbingu/Monrovia Street, opp Jeevanjee Gardens
Kenya Comfort Hotel Suites: Milimani/Ralph Bunche Road
Tel: 020-2716003
www.kenyacomfort.com
Clean, simple accommodation. $–$$

Nairobi Hilton
Mama Ngina Street
Tel: 020-250000
Email: Reservations.Nairobi@hilton.com
In the central shopping and business area of Nairobi. Excellent rooms and cuisine. Heated swimming pool, health club, gym and sauna, ballroom/banqueting facilities, shopping arcade, courtesy shuttle. $$

Nairobi Serena Hotel
Nyerere Road/Kenyatta Avenue
Tel: 020-2822000/2725111
Email: Nairobi@serena.co.ke
Within walking distance of town centre. Excellent pool, gym, sauna, steam bath. $$$

The Norfolk Hotel
Harry Thuku Road
Tel: 020-216964; fax: 020-250200
www.fairmont.com
Central to town. Where the old settlers stayed. Pool, gift shops, hairdressers, travel desk. $$$

Panari Hotel
The Panari Sky Centre
(Mombasa Road, 10 minutes from Airport)
Tel: 020-6946000/828990/3
www.panarihotel.com

practical information

Large, efficient business-style hotel **$$–$$$**

Safari Park Hotel
Thika Road
Tel: 020-3633000/8562222
Email: sales@safaripark.co.ke
Probably the most beautiful hotel in Kenya, all in African style. In extensive landscaped gardens with peacocks and a huge lake-style swimming-pool. 20 minutes from town. **$$**

Upperhill Country Lodge
Second Ngong Avenue
Tel: 020-2881600
www.countrylodge.co.ke
New (November 2006) business-style hotel in quiet location surrounded by gardens. **$$**

Windsor Golf and Country Club
Ridgeways, off Kiambu Road
Tel: 020-8562300/8562500
www.windsorgolfresort.com
Elegant British country club surroundings, about 20 minutes from town. Golf, swimming, jogging track, tennis, gym, beauty parlour, boutiques etc. Excellent restaurant. **$$$**

Nairobi Suburbs
Hotel LaMada
Thika Road
Tel: 020-605328/605067
www.madahotels.com

Some 35 luxury rooms and executive suites on the edge of the Karura forest, 10km (6 miles) from the city centre. **$$**

House of Waine
Masai Lane/Bogani Road, Karen
Tel: 020-891820
www.houseofwaine.co.ke
Chic, luxurious (marble bathrooms etc) in a former private home. **$$$**

Machushla House
Koitobos Road, Langata
Tel: 020-891987
www.macushla.biz
Attractive modern hotel within a short walk of the Giraffe Centre. **$$**

Palacina
Kitale Lane, off Dennis Pritt Road, Milimani
Tel: 020-2715517/8
www.palacina.com
Boutique hotel consisting of The Residence and The Suites – both the height of luxury. Moonflower restaurant is popular with the Nairobi in-crowd. **$$–$$$**

Upcountry
Aberdare Country Club
Outside Mweiga on the B5
Tel: 062-30000/020-216940
www.lonrhohotels.com
A favourite weekend getaway for Nairobi residents. Excellent cuisine, pool, golf

Above: taking it easy by the pool at the Nyali Beach Hotel

course, horse-riding, tennis, trout fishing, gift shop, wildlife sanctuary. **$$$**

Lake Baringo Club
PO Box 40075, Nairobi
Tel: 053-51401/2, 020-4450639
www.blockhotelske.com
On the shore of Lake Baringo, with friendly staff and good food. Pool, games room, bird walks and boating trips (over 460 species of birds recorded). **$$**

Lake Naivasha Country Club
Moi South Lake Road, Naivasha
Tel: 050-2021160/2020925
www.blockhotelske.com
Good food and comfortable accommodation set in 12 hectares (30 acres) of lawns shaded by acacias. Pool, fishing, bird- and hippo-watching on Lake Naivasha. **$$**

Mount Kenya Safari Club
Nanyuki
Tel: 02-216940; fax: 02-216796
www.lonrhohotels.com
Wonderful views of Mount Kenya from this famous club co-founded by film star William Holden. Swimming pool, golf course, bowling green, adjacent to Mount Kenya Game Ranch. **$$$**

Serena Mountain Lodge
Tel: 020-2711077/8
www.serenahotels.com
Wooden lodge built halfway up Mount Kenya surrounded by rainforest, with a water-hole that attracts elephants and much more. **$$**

Mombasa
The best hotels are not on Mombasa Island but on the beaches to the north and south.

Mombasa Serena Beach Hotel
North Beach, Shanzu
Tel: 041-5485721/2
www.serenahotels.com
Swimming, tennis, squash, gift shops, hairdressers, watersports. **$$–$$$**

Nyali Beach Hotel
North Beach
Tel: 041-474640/471567/8
www.nyalibeach.co.ke

Swimming, tennis, golf, squash, hairdressers, gift shops, watersports, six restaurants, disco, car hire desk. **$$**

Voyager Beach Resort
North Coast, Mombasa
PO Box 34177, Mombasa
Tel: 041-475114
www.heritage-eastafrica.com
Family-oriented holiday centre, with 3 pools, 5 restaurants, kids' centre, Adventurers' Club, tennis, games rooms, cyber cafe, gift shop, boutique, hair salon. **$$–$$$**

South Coast
Alliance Jadini Beach Hotel
Diani Beach, South Coast
Tel: 040-320266
www.alliancehotels.com
Swimming, tennis, squash, volleyball, watersports, good restaurants, live evening entertainment. **$$**

Indian Ocean Beach Club
Diani Beach, South Coast
Tel: 040-3203730
www.jacarandahotels.com
Located on a quiet stretch of white sand; swimming, watersports, good restaurants, relaxed atmosphere. **$$**

Leisure Lodge Resort
Diani Beach
Tel: 040-3202011/2
www.leisurelodgeresort.com
Beach and golf resort offering watersports (including diving and deep-sea fishing), 18-hole championship course and a casino. **$$**

Kilifi
Mnarani Club
PO Box 1008, Kilifi Creek
Tel: 041-522318/319
www.mnarani.com
Perched on a cliff overlooking Kilifi Creek and the ocean, an all-inclusive hotel restricted to adults over 16. **$$**

Watamu
Hemingways
Tel: 042-32006
www.hemingways.co.ke
The best hotel on the coast. Excellent service

and food – particularly the smoked sail fish and spicy prawns served (free) at cocktail hour. Uncrowded beach. Few souvenir touts. Deep-sea fishing and water-sports centre. **$$–$$$**

Malindi
Driftwood Beach Club
Silversands Beach
Tel: 042-20155/30569
www.driftwoodclub.com
Good service and facilities, informal atmosphere. Pool, diving centre, squash court, windsurfing, snorkelling. Excellent seafood lunches and moolight barbecues. **$$–$$$**

Home Stays
Some of the best accommodation is on private farms and ranches. Usually these are near, but outside, national parks and reserves, so it's possible to go walking and take night drives (both forbidden in national parks). Some of the properties listed will have rates for both fully catered accommodation and self-catering. Usually there will be staff on hand to do cooking for you, leaving you free to enjoy your surroundings. The farms and ranches below offer 'home stays':

Laikipia
Lolldaiga Hills; Mutamaiyu House; Ol Pejeta Lodge; Segera Ranch House; Laragai Lodge; The Sanctuary at Ol Lentille; Timau River Lodge; Kentrout Cottages; Acacia Homestay, Mweiga; Olea Africana, Mweiga.

Western Kenya
Barnley's House, Kitale; Lokitela Farm, Kitale; Mt Elgon Lodge, Mt Elgon; Rondo Retreat, Kakamega; Kweissos House, Koru; Kembu Cottages, Njoro; Deloraine, Rongai.

Naivasha and Rift Valley
Eburru Guest House; Hippo Point House; Longonot Ranch House; Malu Farm; River House, Gilgil; Hammerkop Roost, Baringo; Rekero Cottages, Maasai Mara.

Coast
Tamarind Village, Mombasa; Shimba Homestead, Shimba Hills; Diani House, Diani; Capricho Cottages, Tiwi Beach; Samawati House, Msambweni; Kikapu Cottages, Watamu; Kingfisher Villa, Malindi; Beach House, Lamu; Palm House, Lamu.

Bookings for the above and more can be made through: **Uniglobe Let's Go Travel**, tel: 020-4447151/4441030; fax: 020-4447270; www.letsgosafari.com; **Exclusive Classic Properties**, tel: 020 7123156; fax: 020 7122638; www.exclusiveclassic properties.com; and **Langata Link**, tel: 020 891665/890699; www.kenyasafari homes.com.

HEALTH & EMERGENCIES

Taking out comprehensive health insurance before you travel to Kenya is very strongly recommended. Ensure also that you visit your doctor well in advance of travelling to discuss/organise taking malaria tablets and having appropriate vaccinations. Also see www. fitfortravel.nhs.uk for more information.

Once in Kenya, if you need hospital treatment go either to Nairobi Hospital (tel: 020-2722160, Argwings Kodhek Road, Nairobi) or Aga Khan University Hospital (tel: 020-3740000, 3rd Parklands Avenue, Nairobi).

In Mombasa, go to the Mombasa Hospital (tel: 041-2312191, off Mama Ngina Drive) or to the Aga Khan Hospital (tel:

Above and right: watersports of all kinds are available at the coast

041-2312953, Vanga Road off Nyrere Avenue). These hospitals are expensive and you must pay a hefty deposit in advance unless you take all your insurance documents with you.

St John's Ambulance can be contacted 24 hours in Nairobi (tel: 020-210000). There is a Coast Ambulance service in Mombasa, tel: 041-3432411.

Air Evacuation

Africa Air Rescue (AAR) provides emergency treatment and air transfer from the bush to a medical centre (office tel: Nairobi 020-2717374, Mombasa 041-2312405/6). **AMREF** (tel: 020-315454/5) also provides a flying doctor service. One month's cover: US$25.

Water

Avoid drinking all tap water – even for cleaning your teeth. Hotels and lodges provide boiled or bottled water for this purpose but even so you may prefer to buy bottled mineral water.

Crime/Security

Poverty and crime are on the increase. Be careful day and night. Wearing expensive jewellery and carrying a camera, camcorder or bulging wallet are easy ways to make yourself a victim. Carry valuables in an old bag and dress down when walking around town. Be careful of strangers who may approach you with 'hard luck' stories. It's best to just say *Pole sana* (pronounced *Polay sarna*, meaning 'I'm very sorry') and walk on. If you do get mugged, hand over whatever is required, avoiding risk of injury.

At night you should take taxis to and from your destination. Keep your car doors locked at all times, even while driving. Valuables and bags should be locked out of sight. Never stop to help broken-down vehicles or to give lifts to strangers. Don't drive after dark and always make sure you are back in Nairobi or your base before sundown.

On safari upcountry, try to travel with more than one vehicle, even if this means making a convoy with strangers.

The **Kenya Tourism Federation (KTF;** KTF Safety and Communication Centre, tel: 020- 601343/605485; fax: 020-604730; mobile: 0722-745645/0733-617499; email: saftourwananchi. com; Mombasa: tel: 041- 887787/316498, mobile: 0722-745644) represents six bodies – the Kenya Association of Tour Operators, Hotel Keepers Association, Kenya Association of Travel Agents, Kenya Association of Air Operators, Budget Hotels and Mombasa & Coast Tourist Association. The KTF's main objective is the safety of tourists in Kenya. To this end, it has a 24-hour Tourist Help Line, which you should call in the event of any security incident, tel: 020-604767

The KTF has three HF radio channels:
10650 Khz Upper Side Band
5853 Khz Lower Side Band
3198 Khz Lower Side Band

This is a 24/7 service with links to the Police, Kenya Wildlife Service, Flying Doctors and members of the tourism industry. You can also call for road and weather conditions.

Police Emergency Telephone Numbers
Nairobi, tel: 999 or 020-240000
Mombasa, tel: 999 or 041-2222121.

TOURIST INFORMATION

Kenya Association of Tour Operators (KATO), tel: 020-2713348/86; www.kato kenya.org.
Kenya Tourist Board, tel: 020-2711262; www.magicalkenya.com.
Mombasa & Coast Tourist Association, tel: 041-225428; mcta@ikenya.com.
Kenya Wildlife Service, tel: 020-600800; www.kws.org.

SPORT

Beach Activities
Windsurfing, kite-surfing, catamaraning, glass-bottom boating and sailing are possible at most hotels down at the coast.

Bungee Jumping
Take a jump over the Tana River (tel: 020-7123094; email: reblin@mitsuminet.com).

Cycling
Bicycles are for hire at most hotels on the coast. For cycling safaris, contact: Let's Go Travel (tel: 020-4447151/1030).

Canoeing
Savage Wilderness Safaris, tel: 020-7121590/0733-735508; www.whitewaterkenya.com.

Deep-Sea Fishing
Beyond the reef enclosing the Kenya coast lie some of the best big game-fishing waters in the world. The fishing season lasts from July to May.

The best places to head out from are Watamu and Malindi in the north or Shimoni to the south. In Watamu, contact Hemingways Deep Sea Fishing and Watersports Centre (tel: 042-32624/32724; fax: 0122-32256; PO Box 267, Watamu; www.hemingways.co.ke). In Malindi, contact the Malindi Deep Sea Fishing Club (tel: 042-20410; PO Box 364, Malindi; email: msfc@swiftmalindi.com). Boats can hold from two to four persons and can go out to sea for a full or half day. It's not cheap (about $560 per boat per day) but it's a great experience.

If you like the idea of trying deep-sea fishing but don't want to kill the fish, Hemingways and many fishermen along the coast also run a tag and release programme for scientific research.

From Shimoni, the Pemba Channel Fishing Club (tel: 040-52016/7; www.pemba channel.com) have four boats for hire, including a 14m (46ft) Sportsfisherman twin diesel 220hp. These boats are also chartered by the Shimoni Reef Lodge (tel: 041-471771, 040-52015; www.oneearthsafaris.com).

Diving
There can be few better places to learn how to dive than Diani, Watamu, Shimoni or Malindi, and internationally recognised Professional Association of Diving Instructors (PADI) courses can be arranged at most hotels. You'll spend the first day getting used to the equipment and learning safety procedures in a swimming-pool. After that you'll be out diving off the reef. It takes four days to complete the open water course. You can also take the advanced course (three days), rescue diver course (minimum seven days) or dive master course (minimum two weeks).

If you're an experienced diver, the underwater cliffs in the clear seas off Shimoni are renowned for their diversity of marine

Left: angler's prize – a giant Nile perch

life. There are also underwater caves in Mida Creek to the south of Watamu which are home to giant rock cod *(tewa)* weighing up to 400kg (880lb) but beware – the underwater currents can be very strong.

Snorkelling

The best snorkelling is in the Kisite-Mpunguti Marine Reserve off Shimoni in the south *(see Itinerary 21, page 59)* where the water is crystal clear and the coral is still fairly undisturbed.

The Watamu Marine Reserve in the north is a good second-best. Conservationists are concerned that siltation from the Sabaki river north of Malindi is slowly suffocating the coral polyps and preventing them from feeding. For the time being, though, there are plenty of fish and marine flora.

Freshwater Fishing

At Naivasha, contact Lake Naivasha Country Club (tel: 050-2021160/2020925; email: reservations@kenyahotelsltd.com); in the Aberdares, contact Aberdare Country Club (tel: 061-55620 or 02-216940); in Nanyuki, contact Mount Kenya Safari Club (tel: 062-30000). On Lake Victoria, contact Rusinga Island Lodge (tel: 020-882028/222598).

Fly-fishing safaris are becoming increasingly popular and Kenya has a wide range of fishing locations, from the cold highland streams of the Aberdares to the Indian Ocean. Contact: www.flyfishingkenya.com.

Golf

There are 40 golf courses in Kenya, and tailor-made safaris for the enthusiastic golfer are easily organised (www.kenya-golf-safaris.com). There are five courses in and around Nairobi: Karen Golf Club (tel: 020-882801/2; www.karencountryclub.org); Muthaiga Golf Club (tel: 020-3762414; email: muthaiga@wananchi.com); Royal Nairobi Golf Club (tel: 020-2712521); Limuru Country Club (tel: 066-73338) and Windsor Golf and Country Club (tel: 020-8562300/500; www.windsorgolfresort.com).

Among the highly rated up-country courses are: Great Rift Valley Lodge (tel: 050-50047/8; www.heritage-eastafrica.com); Aberdare Country Club (tel: 061-55620/020-216940; www.lonrhohotels.com); Nanyuki

Sports Club (tel: 062-31896; email: nanyukisc@africaonline.co.ke); Eldoret Sports Club (tel: 053-2031395/2031249); Nyanza Club (tel: 057-2024058/2020783; email: nyanzaclub@africaonline.co.ke).

One the coast, your hotel will be able to advise you on golf courses. Among the best are: Mombasa Golf Club, Mombasa Island (tel: 041-2228531; email: mombasagolf@wananchi.com); Leisure Golf Club, Diani Beach (tel: 040-3202620/3202011; www.leisurelodgeresort.com); Nyali Golf & Country Club (tel: 041-472632/471589; email: nyaligolf@wananchi.com); and Malindi Golf & Country Club (tel: 042-31402);

Tennis

In Nairobi, play at the Nairobi Club in Ngong Road (tel: 020-2725726-29; email: nairobiclub@iconnect.co.ke), at Windsor Golf and Country Club *(see Golf)* and Limuru Country Club *(see Golf)*. Many hotels have their own courts. There are also plenty of courts in Mombasa. Check with your hotel.

Horse-riding

Join a full- or half-day trek from Karen to the edge of the Rift Valley with Nkudzi Riding School, Ngong Road, Karen (tel: 020-882512/0733-606024). Horseback safaris on the perimeter of the Maasai Mara can be organised through Tony Church at Safaris Unlimited (tel: 020-891976/890435; www.safarisunlimited.com).

Walking

Walking is generally not permitted in the National Parks and National Reserves, but walking safaris in the region outside the Maasai Mara and in northern Kenya can be organised through Let's Go Travel (tel: 020-4447151/4441030; www.letsgosafari.com).

Waterskiing

Most hotels on the coast offer waterskiing. You can also ski on Lakes Naivasha and Baringo and in Mida Creek behind Watamu. In Naivasha, contact Lake Naivasha Country Club *(see Freshwater fishing)*; in Baringo, contact Island Camp *(see Itinerary 10, page 36)*; in Watamu, contact Hemingways Deep Sea Fishing and Watersports Centre *(see Deep Sea Fishing)*.

Whitewater Rafting

To raft down the Athi or Tana river, on safaris lasting from one day to two weeks or more, contact Savage Wilderness Safaris Ltd (tel: 020-7121590/0733-735508; www. whitewaterkenya.com).

USEFUL INFORMATION

Photography

Slide and print film and processing facilities are widely available. Don't forget to bring a spare camera battery, a lens hood, ultra-violet filter and a telephoto lens (200–300mm). It can get very dusty on safari so a good camera bag is useful. In Nairobi, Expo Camera Centre on Mama Ngina Street (tel: 020-221797/3752821) repair cameras and hire out equipment.

Digital cameras and video recorders are greedy for batteries. Be sure to bring plenty of spares or, better still, rechargeable batteries and a charger. Most camps and lodges provide a facility for recharging batteries overnight, but always check in advance.

Maps

The pullout map in the wallet at the back of this book plots the itineraries in colour. Other useful maps are the Macmillan Travellers' maps of Maasai Mara National Reserve, Amboseli, and Tsavo East and West National Parks. Tourist Maps (K) Ltd publish maps of Lake Nakuru National Park and a Nairobi map.

Bookshops

There are a number of good bookshops in Nairobi. One of the best is the Stanley Bookshop (tel: 020-212776) on the corner of Kenyatta Avenue and Moi Avenue, just round from the Stanley Hotel.

Also very good are The Text Book Centre (tel: 020-4449680/1) in the Sarit Centre, Westlands, the Village Bookshop at the Village Market (tel: 020-7122437) and Westland Sundries (tel: 020-4446406/8998) in Old Uchumi House, Westlands Road; Books First at Ukay Centre, Westlands; Nakumatt at Uhuru Highway, Village Market, Prestige Centre and The Junction Shopping Centre, Ngong Road; Book Stop at Yaya Centre,

Argwings Kodhek Road (tel: 020-2714533/47); and Nu Metro Media Store, The Junction Shopping Centre, Ngong Road (tel: 020-3878484/5/6).

Consulates

Australia Riverside Drive, PO Box 34341, Nairobi; tel: 020-4445034-9.

Canada Limuru Road, Gigiri, PO Box 1013, 00621 Village Market, Nairobi; tel: 020-3663000.

France Barclays Plaza, Loita Stree, PO Box 41784, 00100 GPO, Nairobi; tel: 020-316363; fax: 02-217013; www.ambafrance-ke.org.

Germany 113 Riverside Drive, PO Box 30180, 00100 GPO, Nairobi; tel: 020-4262000; email: info@nairobi.diplo.de.

Italy International Life House, Mama Ngina Street, PO Box 30107, 00100, Nairobi; tel: 020-247750/247696.

Spain Bruce House, Standard Street, PO Box 45503, 00100, Nairobi; tel: 020-342232/28.

UK Upper Hill Road, PO Box 30465, 00100, Nairobi; tel: 020-2844000; email: bhcinfo@iconnect.co.ke.

USA United Nations Avenue, Nairobi; tel: 020-3636000; fax: 020-3636157.

LANGUAGE

Useful Kiswahili phrases

Hello	*Jambo*
How are you?	*Habari gani?*
Fine/very well/good	*Mzuri*
Bad	*Mbaya*
Thank you (very much)	*Asante (sana)*
Please	*Tafadhali*
Goodbye	*Kwaheri*
Welcome	*Karibu*
Sorry	*Pole*
Very	*Sana*
Who?	*Nani?*
What?	*Nini?*
Where?	*Wapi?*
When?	*Lini?*
Why?	*Kwa nini?*
How?	*Vipi?*
A lot	*Nyingi*
More	*Ngine*

Today	*Leo*	Expensive	*Ghali*
Tomorrow	*Kesho*	Money	*Pesa*
Now	*Sasa*	Shop	*Duka*
Yes	*Ndiyo*	Market	*Soko*
No	*Hapana*		

Phrases

Good morning	*Habari ya asabuhi?*
reply:	*Mzuri, asante*
What is your name?	*Jina lako nani?*
My name is...	*Jina langu ni...*
Right	*Kulia*
Left	*Kushoto*
Straight ahead	*Moja ku moja*
Wait a minute	*Ngoja kidogo*
Where is the toilet?	*Choo iko wapi?*

Food and drink

Food	*Chakula*
Drink	*Kinwaje*
Coffee	*Kahawa*
Tea	*Chai*
Milk	*Maziwa*
Water	*Maji*
Sugar	*Sukari*
Cold	*Baridi*
Beer/alcohol	*Pombe*
Small	*Kidogo*
Big	*Kubwa*
Meat	*Nyama*
Fruit	*Matunda*
Fish	*Samaki*

Numbers

1	*Moja*	6	*Sita*
2	*Mbili*	7	*Saba*
3	*Tatu*	8	*Nane*
4	*Nne*	9	*Tisa*
5	*Tano*	10	*Kumi*

11	*Kumi na moja*
12	*Kumi na mbili* etc
20	*Ishirini*
21	*Ishirini na moja* etc
30	*Thelathini*
40	*Arobaini*
50	*Hamsini*
100	*Mia moja*
1,000	*Elfu moja*

Shopping

How much?	*Bei gani?* or
	Pesa ngapi?

FURTHER READING

Insight Guide: Kenya and *Insight Guide: East African Wildlife*. Apa Publications.

The Beauty of the Maasai Mara, David Round-Turner; 1994

The Beauty of Amboseli, Jan Hemsing, M. Amin; 1995

The Beauty of Samburu, Jan Hemsing, M. Amin; 1997

The Beautiful People of Kenya, Amin, Willets & Tetley; 1995

Big Cat Diary: Leopard/Lion, Jonathan & Angela Scott; BBC

Flame Trees of Thika, Elspeth Huxley; 1987

Johnathan Scott's Safari Guide to Eastern African Birds; 1997

Kenya: The Magic Land, Amin, Willetts and Tetley; London 1988.

A Leopard's Tale, *Kingdom of Lions*, Jonathan Scott

The Lions of Tsavo, Bruce D. Patterson; McGraw-Hill; 2001

My Kenya Days, Wilfred Thesiger.

Nine Faces of Kenya, Elspeth Huxley (ed); London 1991.

Out of Africa, Karen Blixen; 1938.

Peoples of Kenya, Joy Adamson; London 1967.

Portraits of Kenya, Moll Amin; Nairobi 1995.

White Mischief, James Fox; New York 1994.

Right: wildlife always has right of way

c r e d i t s

ACKNOWLEDGEMENTS

10, 12T, 13, 71, 73, 74	**Mohamed Amin & Duncan Willets**
23, 32, 35, 36, 43T, 49, 55, 62, 79, 92, 93	**Bodo Bondzio**
82	**Zdenka Bondzio**
76	**Camerapix**
94	**Peter Davey**
6T, 7T, 7B, 11, 30, 33T, 42, 43B, 45, 46, 66, 69, 78, 80, 81, 83, 89, 90, 98	**Glyn Genin**
52	**Chris Howes/Wild Places Photography/ Alamy**
1, 2/3, 6B, 12B, 14, 15, 16, 21, 24, 25, 27B, 28, 29, 31T, 31B, 33B, 34, 37, 38, 39, 40, 41, 47, 48, 57. 59T, 59B, 63, 68, 75	**David Keith Jones/Images of Africa**
53	**Kirsty Mclaren/Alamy**
50	**Nature Picture Library/Alamy**
22	**Stan Oslinski/Corbis**
8/9	**Nigel Pavitt/John Warburton Lee**
20	**Radu Sigheti/Reuters/Corbis**
27T, 54, 56, 60, 61T, 61B, 67, 70	**Wendy Stone**
64	**Ken Walsh/Alamy**
5, 97	**Marcus Wilson-Smith**
Cartography	**Maria Donnelly Berndtson & Berndtson**
Cover	**Art Wolfe/Getty Images**

INSIGHT CITY GUIDES

The Guides That Are Streets Ahead

*Insight Guides to every major country
are also available*

www.insightguides.com

INDEX